A Christian Manifesto

By Francis A. Schaeffer

FRANCIS A. SCHAEFFER

A
Christian
Manifesto

CROSSWAY BOOKS • WHEATON, ILLINOIS
A DIVISION OF GOOD NEWS PUBLISHERS

PUBLISHED IN ASSOCIATION WITH
NIMS COMMUNICATIONS

Dedication

To all those who have said: "Here I stand" facing oppressive authoritarian civil and church power.

There were Peter and John who said to the Sanhedrin: "Judge for yourselves whether it is right in God's sight to obey you rather than God." (Acts 4:19)

There were the Reformers of the sixteenth century when they had to decide whether they were going to obey God or man.

And most of all, to Samuel Rutherford. He has meant much to me for many years, but especially so from the time I began working on the material for the book and films *How Should We Then Live?* At that time I understood increasingly that Samuel Rutherford's *Lex Rex* was an important trailmarker for our day. In the times I have spoken at St. Andrews University, the most outstanding thing for me was a feeling that Samuel Rutherford was not far away, that the old Rector was close by, and very contemporary!

Contents

Preface

This book is the natural outgrowth of the books which have gone before. The earliest books, *The God Who Is There, Escape From Reason,* and *He Is There and He Is Not Silent,* dealt with the Lordship of Christ over all of life—philosophy, theology and the church, art, music, literature, films, and culture in general. The books that followed dealt with and extended areas of Christ's total Lordship in all of life, and my wife Edith's books added to that extension and expansion.

With the most recent books and their accompanying film series, I, and all of us working together on these, carried the Lordship of Christ in the whole spectrum of life further. *How Should We Then Live?* dealt with the area of history and with the shifts which have come in society, government, and law. *Whatever Happened to the Human Race?*, written and filmed with

9

Dr. C. Everett Koop, dealt with how modern, arbitrary law and modern and humanistic medicine have met at the crucial point of human life.

That led to the demand of the next logical step: What is the Christian's relationship to government, law, and civil disobedience?

At that point, Jerry Nims, who with his family had come to study in L'Abri, began to ask penetrating questions concerning these things. We had long talks and he urged me to put my answers into written form. Without that impetus there would have been no book.

Then Franky Schaeffer V entered and put together the basic publishing package as well as providing ideas and concepts in long times of talking and adding to the early draft of a possible text.

During this same period Franky, Jim Buchfuehrer, Edith, and I had been working on a new film series, *Reclaiming the World* (Franky Schaeffer V Productions). As Franky, Dr. Jeremy Jackson, Edith, and I discussed the pressing questions of the day before the camera, ideas about the Christian's relationship to government and law (among many other subjects) were sharpened and focused.

Then John Whitehead, an attorney-at-law, gave certain invaluable suggestions and ideas for which I am deeply appreciative.

Finally, the skeleton of the book emerged on the basis of a talk I gave at a plenary session of the Christian Legal Society Conference in South Bend on April 24, 1981. The discussion period following the lecture with the attending lawyers stirred my thinking further. Since the talk I have read many legal briefs and records of specific cases. The talk I gave at the Conference is enlarged into the present form and includes all I have been reading and thinking about in this area for many years, the material I have been especially gathering over the last year, and the input I have spoken of above.

The book is written not as a theoretical exercise but as a *manifesto*.

For additional reading, do pursue the books and films mentioned in the text. They are listed at the end of this book. A film entitled *The Second American Revolution*, being made by Franky Schaeffer V Productions, will be a special help.

Of course, there are many helpful books, but I would especially suggest these:

The Second American Revolution by John W. Whitehead documents in detail the root causes of the humanist dominance in the West while focusing on the emergence of the judicial and governmental authoritarian elite in the United States. It also discusses Christian resistance in light of unbiblical state actions.

No Other Foundation by Jeremy Jackson offers a solid study of church history which is not a series of dry facts but which relates past history to lessons to be learned for the present problems facing the church.

Addicted to Mediocrity by Franky Schaeffer V speaks practically concerning the truncated view of culture which a false and unbiblical pietism has caused.

These last two books, and this volume as well, are published by Crossway Books. We appreciate Lane Dennis at Crossway, who has worked closely with us on format and design to produce books not only of beauty, but books that deal with the hard areas where Christians will or will not confront today's increasingly broken and inhuman world.

And I do want to say thank you to my wife, Edith, for her sensitivity concerning the many difficult balances involved in this present book; to Udo Middelmann for his positive criticism; to Jeremy Jackson for help concerning historical details; and to Jim and Gail Ingram, without whose help I never could have made the publisher's deadline.

Francis A. Schaeffer
Switzerland, 1981

The Communist Manifesto 1848
Humanist Manifesto I 1933
Humanist Manifesto II 1973

A Christian Manifesto

CHAPTER ONE
The Abolition of Truth and Morality

The basic problem of the Christians in this country in the last eighty years or so, in regard to society and in regard to government, is that they have seen things in bits and pieces instead of totals.

They have very gradually become disturbed over permissiveness, pornography, the public schools, the breakdown of the family, and finally abortion. But they have not seen this as a totality—each thing being a part, a symptom, of a much larger problem. They have failed to see that all of this has come about due to a shift in world view—that is, through a fundamental change in the overall way people think and view the world and life as a whole. This shift has been *away from* a world view that was at least vaguely Christian in people's memory (even if they were not individually Christian) *toward* something completely different—toward a world view based upon the idea that the final reality is impersonal matter or energy shaped into its present form by impersonal chance. They have not seen that this world view has taken the place of the one that had previously dominated Northern European culture, including the United States, which was at least Christian in memory, even if the individuals were not individually Christian.

These two world views stand as totals in complete antithesis to each other in content and also in their natural results—including sociological and governmental results, and specifically including law.

It is not that these two world views are different only in how they understand the nature of reality and existence. They also inevitably produce totally different results. The operative word here is *inevitably*. It is not just that they happen to bring forth different results, but it is absolutely *inevitable* that they will bring forth different results.

Why have the Christians been so slow to understand this? There are various reasons but the central one is a defective view of Christianity. This has its roots in the Pietist movement under the leadership of P. J. Spener in the seventeenth century. Pietism began as a healthy protest against formalism and a too abstract Christianity. But it had a deficient, "platonic" spirituality. It was platonic in the sense that Pietism made a sharp division between the "spiritual" and the "material" world—giving little, or no, importance to the "material" world. The totality of human existence was not afforded a proper place. In particular it neglected the intellectual dimension of Christianity.

Christianity and spirituality were shut up to a small, isolated part of life. The totality of reality was ignored by the pietistic thinking. Let me quickly say that in one sense Christians should be pietists in that Christianity is not just a set of doctrines, even the right doctrines. *Every* doctrine is in some way to have an effect upon our lives. But the poor side of Pietism and its resulting platonic outlook has really been a tragedy not only in many people's individual lives, but in our total culture.

True spirituality covers all of reality. There are things the Bible tells us as absolutes which are sinful— which do not conform to the character of God. But aside from these the Lordship of Christ covers *all* of life and *all* of life equally. It is not only that true spirituality covers all of life, but it covers all parts of the spectrum of life equally. In this sense there is nothing concerning reality that is not spiritual.

Related to this, it seems to me, is the fact that many Christians do not mean what I mean when I say Christianity is true, or Truth. They are Christians and they believe in, let us say, the truth of creation, the truth of the virgin birth, the truth of Christ's miracles, Christ's substitutionary death, and His coming again. But they stop there with these and other individual truths.

When I say Christianity is true I mean it is true to

19

total reality—the total of what is, beginning with the central reality, the objective existence of the personal-infinite God. Christianity is not just a series of truths but *Truth*—Truth about all of reality. And the holding to that Truth intellectually—and then in some poor way living upon that Truth, the Truth of what is—brings forth not only certain personal results, but also governmental and legal results.

Now let's go over to the other side—to those who hold the materialistic final reality concept. They saw the complete and total difference between the two positions more quickly than Christians. There were the Huxleys, George Bernard Shaw (1856-1950), and many others who understood a long time ago that there are two total concepts of reality and that it was one total reality against the other and not just a set of isolated and separated differences. The *Humanist Manifesto I*,[1] published in 1933, showed with crystal clarity their comprehension of the totality of what is involved. It was to our shame that Julian (1887-1975) and Aldous Huxley (1894-1963), and the others like them, understood much earlier than Christians that these two world views are two total concepts of reality standing in antithesis to each other. We should be utterly ashamed that this is the fact.

They understood not only that there were two totally different concepts but that they would bring forth two totally different conclusions, both for individuals and for society. What we must understand is that the two world views really do bring forth with inevitable certainty not only personal differences, but also total differences in regard to society, government, and law.

There is no way to mix these two total world views. They are separate entities that cannot be synthesized. Yet we must say that liberal theology, the very essence of it from its beginning, is an attempt to mix the two. Liberal theology tried to bring forth a mixture soon after the Enlightenment and has tried to synthesize these two views right up to our own day. But in each case when the chips are down these liberal theologians have always come down, as naturally as a ship coming into home port, on the side of the nonreligious humanist. They do this with certainty because what their liberal theology really is is humanism expressed in theological terms instead of philosophic or other terms.

An example of this coming down naturally on the side of the nonreligious humanists is the article by Charles Hartshorne in the January 21, 1981, issue of *The Christian Century*, pages 42-45. Its title is, "Concerning Abortion, an Attempt at a Rational View." He begins by equating the fact that the human fetus is alive with the fact that mosquitoes and bacteria are also alive. That is, he begins by assuming that human life is not unique. He then continues by saying that *even after the baby is born* it is not fully human until its social relations develop (though he says the infant does have some primitive social relations an unborn

21

fetus does not have). His conclusion is, "Nevertheless, I have little sympathy with the idea that infanticide is just another form of murder. Persons who are already functionally persons in the full sense have more important rights even than infants." He then, logically, takes the next step: "Does this distinction apply to the killing of a hopelessly senile person or one in a permanent coma? For me it does." No atheistic humanist could say it with greater clarity. It is significant at this point to note that many of the denominations controlled by liberal theology have come out, publicly and strongly, in favor of abortion.

Dr. Martin E. Marty is one of the respected, theologically liberal spokesmen. He is an associate editor of *The Christian Century* and Fairfax M. Cone distinguished service professor at the University of Chicago divinity school. He is often quoted in the secular press as the spokesman for "mainstream" Christianity. In a *Christian Century* article in the January 7-14, 1981, issue (pages 13-17 with an addition on page 31), he has an article entitled: "Dear Republicans: A Letter on Humanisms." In it he brilliantly confuses the terms "being human," humanism, the humanities and being "in love with humanity." Why does he do this? As a historian he knows the distinctions of those words, but when one is done with these pages the poor reader who knows no better is left with the eradication of the total distinction between the Christian position and the humanist one. I admire the cleverness of the arti-

22

cle, but I regret that in it Dr. Marty has come down on the nonreligious humanist side, by confusing the issues so totally.

It would be well at this point to stress that we should not confuse the very different things which Dr. Marty did confuse. *Humanitarianism* is being kind and helpful to people, treating people humanly. The *humanities* are the studies of literature, art, music, etc.—those things which are the products of human creativity. *Humanism* is the placing of Man at the center of all things and making him the measure of all things.

Thus, Christians should be the most humanitarian of all people. And Christians certainly should be interested in the humanities as the product of human creativity, made possible because people are uniquely made in the image of the great Creator. In this sense of being interested in the humanities it would be proper to speak of a Christian humanist. This is especially so in the past usage of that term. This would then mean that such a Christian is interested (as we all should be) in the product of people's creativity. In this sense, for example, Calvin could be called a Christian humanist because he knew the works of the Roman writer Seneca so very well.[2] John Milton and many other Christian poets could also be so called because of their knowledge not only of their own day but also of antiquity.

But in contrast to being humanitarian and being interested in the humanities Christians should be in-

alterably opposed to the false and destructive humanism, which is false to the Bible and equally false to
what Man is.

Along with this we must keep distinct the "humanist world view" of which we have been speaking and
such a thing as the "Humanist Society," which produced the Humanist Manifestos I and II (1933 and
1973). The Humanist Society is made up of a relative-
ly small group of people (some of whom, however,
have been influential—John Dewey, Sir Julian Huxley, Jacques Monod, B. F. Skinner, etc.). By way of
contrast, the humanist world view includes many
thousands of adherents and today controls the consensus
in society, much of the media, much of what is taught in
our schools, and much of the arbitrary law being produced
by the various departments of government.

The term humanism used in this wider, more preva-
lent way means Man beginning from himself, with no
knowledge except what he himself can discover and
no standards outside of himself. In this view Man is
the measure of all things, as the Enlightenment expressed it.

Nowhere have the divergent results of the two total
concepts of reality, the Judeo-Christian and the humanist world view, been more open to observation
than in government and law.

We of Northern Europe (and we must remember
that the United States, Canada, Australia, New Zea-

land and so on are extensions of Northern Europe)
take our *form-freedom balance* in government for
granted as though it were natural. There is form in
acknowledging the obligations in society, and there is
freedom in acknowledging the rights of the individual.
We have form, we have freedom; there is freedom,
there is form. There is a balance here which we have
come to take as natural in the world. It is not natural
in the world. We are utterly foolish if we look at the
long span of history and read the daily newspapers
giving today's history and do not understand that the
form-freedom balance in government which we have
had in Northern Europe since the Reformation and in
the countries extended from it is unique in the world,
past and present.

That is not to say that no one wrestled with these
questions before the Reformation nor that no one produced anything worthwhile. One can think, for example, of the Conciliar Movement in the late medieval
church and the early medieval parliaments.[3] Especially one must consider the ancient English Common
Law. And in relation to that Common Law (and all
English Law) there is Henry De Bracton. I will men-
tion more about him in a moment.

Those who hold the material-energy, chance concept of reality, whether they are Marxist or non-
Marxist, not only do not know the truth of the final
reality, God, they do not know who Man is. Their
concept of Man is what Man is not, just as their con-

25

cept of the final reality is what final reality is not. Since their concept of Man is mistaken, their concept of society and of law is mistaken, and they have no sufficient base for either society or law.

They have reduced Man to even less than his natural finiteness by seeing him only as a complex arrangement of molecules, made complex by blind chance. Instead of seeing him as something great who is significant even in his sinning, they see Man in his essence only as an intrinsically competitive animal, that has no other basic operating principle than natural selection brought about by the strongest, the fittest, ending on top. And they see Man as acting in this way both individually and collectively as society.

Even on the basis of Man's finiteness having people swear in court *in the name of humanity*, as some have advocated, saying something like, "We pledge our honor before all mankind"[4] would be insufficient enough. But reduced to the materialistic view of Man, it is even less. Although many nice words may be used, in reality law constituted on this basis can only mean brute force.

In this setting Jeremy Bentham's (1748-1842) Utilitarianism can be and must be all that law means. And this must inevitably lead to the conclusion of Oliver Wendell Holmes Jr. (1841-1935): "The life of the law has not been logic: it has been experience."[5] That is, there is *no* basis for law except Man's limited, finite experience. And especially with the Darwinian, survival-of-the-fittest concept of Man (which Holmes held) that must, and will, lead to Holmes' final conclusion: law is "the majority vote of that nation that could lick all others."[6]

The problem always was, and is, What is an adequate base for law? What is adequate so that the human aspiration for freedom can exist without anarchy, and yet provides a form that will not become arbitrary tyranny?

In contrast to the materialistic concept, Man in reality is made in the image of God and has real humanness. This humanness has produced varying degrees of success in government, bringing forth governments that were more than only the dominance of brute force.

And those in the stream of the Judeo-Christian world view have had something more. The influence of the Judeo-Christian world view can be perhaps most readily observed in Henry De Bracton's influence on British Law. An English judge living in the thirteenth century, he wrote *De Legibus et Consuetudinibus* (c. 1250).

Bracton, in the stream of the Judeo-Christian world view, said:

And that he [the King] ought to be under the law appears clearly in the analogy of Jesus Christ, whose vice-regent on earth he is, for though many ways were open to Him for His ineffable redemption of the human race, the true mercy of God chose this most powerful way to destroy the devil's

27

work, he would not use the power of force but the reason of justice.[7,8]

In other words, God in His sheer power could have crushed Satan in his revolt by the use of that sufficient power. But because of God's character, justice came before the use of power alone. Therefore Christ died that justice, rooted in what God is, would be the solution. Bracton codified this: Christ's example, because of who He is, is our standard, our rule, our measure. Therefore power is not first, but justice is first in society and law. The prince may have the power to control and to rule, but he does not have the right to do so without justice. This was the basis of English Common Law. The Magna Charta (1215) was written within thirty-five years (or less) of Bracton's *De Legibus* and in the midst of the same universal thinking in England at that time.

The Reformation (300 years after Bracton) refined and clarified this further. It got rid of the encrustations that had been added to the Judeo-Christian world view and clarified the point of authority—with authority resting in the Scripture rather than church *and* Scripture, or state *and* Scripture. This not only had meaning in regard to doctrine but clarified the base for law.

That base was God's written Law, back through the New Testament to Moses' written Law; and the content and authority of that written Law is rooted back to Him who is the final reality. Thus, neither church

28

nor state were equal to, let alone above, that Law. The base for law is not divided, and no one has the right to place anything, including king, state or church, above the content of God's Law.

What the Reformation did was to return most clearly and consistently to the origins, to the final reality, God; but equally to the reality of Man—not only Man's personal needs (such as salvation), but also Man's social needs.

What we have had for four hundred years, produced from this clarity, is unique in contrast to the situation that has existed in the world in forms of government. Some of you have been taught that the Greek city states had our concepts in government. It simply is not true.[9] All one has to do is read Plato's *Republic* to have this come across with tremendous force.

When the men of our State Department, especially after World War II, went all over the world trying to implant our form-freedom balance in government downward on cultures whose philosophy and religion would never have produced it, it has, in almost every case, ended in some form of totalitarianism or authoritarianism.

The humanists push for "freedom," but having no Christian consensus to contain it, that "freedom" leads to chaos or to slavery under the state (or under an elite). Humanism, with its lack of *any* final base for values or law, always leads to chaos. It then naturally leads to some form of authoritarianism to control the chaos. Having produced the sickness, humanism gives more of the same kind of medicine for a cure. With its mistaken concept of final reality, it has no intrinsic reason to be interested in the individual, the human being. Its natural interest is the two collectives: the state and society.

CHAPTER TWO

Foundations for Faith and Freedom

The Founding Fathers of the United States (in varying degrees) understood very well the relationship between one's world view and government. John Witherspoon (1723-1794) has always been important to me personally, and he is even more so since I have read just recently a biography of him by David Walker Woods.[1] John Witherspoon, a Presbyterian minister and president of what is now Princeton University, was the only pastor to sign the Declaration of Independence. He was a very important man during the founding of the country. He linked the Christian thinking represented by the College of New Jersey (now Princeton University) with the work he did both on the Declaration of Independence and on countless very important committees in the founding of the country. This linkage of Christian thinking and the concepts of government were not incidental but fundamental. John Witherspoon knew and stood consciously in the stream of Samuel Rutherford, a Scotsman who lived from 1600-1661 and who wrote *Lex Rex* in 1644. *Lex rex* means law is king—a phrase that was absolutely earthshaking. Prior to that it had been *rex lex*, the king is law. In *Lex Rex* he wrote that the law, and no one else, is king. Therefore, the heads of government are under the law, not a law unto themselves.

Jefferson, who was a deist, and others, knew they stood in the stream of John Locke (1632-1704), and while Locke had secularized *Lex Rex* he had drawn heavily from it. These men really knew what they were doing. We are not reading back into history what was not there. We cannot say too strongly that they really understood the basis of the government which they were founding. Think of this great flaming phrase: "certain inalienable rights." Who gives the rights? The state? Then they are not inalienable because the state can change them and take them away. Where do the rights come from? They understood that they were founding the country upon the concept that goes back into the Judeo-Christian thinking that there is Someone there who gave the inalienable rights. Another phrase also stood there: "In God we trust." With this there is no confusion of what they were talking about. They publicly recognized that law could be king because there was a Law Giver, a Person to give the inalienable rights.

Most people do not realize that there was a paid chaplain in Congress even before the Revolutionary War ended. Also we find that prior to the founding of the national congress all the early provincial congresses in all thirteen colonies always opened with prayer. And from the very beginning, prayer opened the national congress. These men truly understood what they were doing. They knew they were building on the Supreme Being who was the Creator, the final reality. And they knew that without that foundation everything in the Declaration of Independence and all that followed would be sheer unadulterated nonsense. These were brilliant men who understood exactly what was involved.

As soon as the war was over they called the first Thanksgiving Day. Do you realize that the first Thanksgiving Day to thank God in this country was called immediately by the Congress at the end of the war? Witherspoon's sermon on that day shows their perspective: "A republic once equally poised must either preserve its virtue or lose its liberty." Don't you wish that everybody in America would recite that, and truly understand it, every morning? "A republic once equally poised must either preserve its virtue or lose its liberty." Earlier in a speech Witherspoon had stressed: "He is the best friend of American liberty who is most sincere and active in promoting pure and undefiled religion." And for Witherspoon, and the cultural consensus of that day, that meant Christianity as it had come to them through the Reformation. This was the consensus which then gave religious freedom to all— including the "free thinkers" of that day and the humanists of our day.

This concept was the same as William Penn (1644-1718) had expressed earlier: "If we are not governed by God, then we will be ruled by tyrants." This consensus was as natural as breathing in the United States at that time. We must not forget that many of those who came to America from Europe came for religious purposes. As they arrived, most of them established their own individual civil governments based upon the Bible. It is, therefore, totally foreign to the basic nature of America at the time of the writing of the Constitution to argue a separation doctrine that implies a secular state.

When the First Amendment was passed it only had two purposes. The first purpose was that there would be no established, national church for the united thirteen states. To say it another way: There would be no "Church of the United States." James Madison (1751-1836) clearly articulated this concept of separation when explaining the First Amendment's protection of religious liberty. He said that the First Amendment to the Constitution was prompted because "the people feared one sect might obtain a preeminence, or two combine together, and establish a religion to which they would compel others to conform."[2]

Nevertheless, a number of the individual states had state churches, and even that was not considered in conflict with the First Amendment. "At the outbreak of the American Revolution, nine of the thirteen colonies had conferred special benefits upon one church to the exclusion of others."[3] "In all but one of the thirteen states, the states taxed the people to support the preaching of the gospel and to build churches."[4] "It was not until 1798 that the Virginia legislature repealed all its laws supporting churches."[5] "In Massachusetts the Massachusetts Constitution was not amended until 1853 to eliminate the tax-supported church provisions."[6]

The second purpose of the First Amendment was the very opposite from what is being made of it today. It states expressly that government should not impede or interfere with the free practice of religion.

Those were the two purposes of the First Amendment as it was written.

As Justice Douglas wrote for the majority of the Supreme Court in the United States v. Ballard case in 1944:

The First Amendment has a dual aspect. It not only "forestalls compulsion by law of the acceptance of any creed or the practice of any form of worship" but also "safeguards the free exercise of the chosen form of religion."

Today the separation of church and state in America is used to silence the church. When Christians speak out on issues, the hue and cry from the humanist state and media is that Christians, and all religions, are prohibited from speaking since there is a separation of church and state. The way the concept is used today is totally reversed from the original intent. It is not rooted in history. The modern concept of separation is an argument for a total separation of religion from the state. The consequence of the acceptance of this doctrine leads to the removal of religion as an influence in civil government. This fact is well illustrated by John W. Whitehead in his book *The Second American Revolution*.[7] It is used today as a false political dictum in order to restrict the influence of Christian ideas. As Franky Schaeffer V says in the *Plan for Action*:

It has been convenient and expedient for the secular humanist, the materialist, the so-called liberal, the feminist, the genetic engineer, the bureaucrat, the Supreme Court Justice, to use this arbitrary division between church and state as a ready excuse. It is used, as an easily identifiable rallying point, to subdue the opinions of that vast body of citizens who represent those with religious convictions.[8]

To have suggested the state separated from religion and religious influence would have amazed the Founding Fathers. The French Revolution that took place shortly afterwards, with its continuing excesses and final failure leading quickly to Napoleon and an authoritative rule, only emphasized the difference between the base upon which the United States was founded and the base upon which the French Revolution was founded. History is clear and the men of that day understood it. Terry Eastland said in *Commentary* magazine:

As a matter of historical fact, the Founding Fathers believed that the public interest was served by the promotion of religion. The Northwest Ordinance of 1787, which set aside federal property in the territory for schools and which was passed again by Congress in 1789, is instructive. "Religion, morality, and knowledge being necessary to good government and the happiness of mankind," read the act, "schools and the means of learning shall forever be encouraged." . . .

In 1811 the New York state court upheld an indictment for blasphemous utterances against Christ, and in its ruling, given by Chief Justice Kent, the court said, "We are Christian people, and the morality of the country is deeply engrafted upon Christianity." Fifty years later this same court said that "Christianity may be conceded to be the established religion."

The Pennsylvania state court also affirmed the conviction of a man on charges of blasphemy, here against the Holy Scriptures. The Court said: "Christianity, general Christianity is, and always has been, a part of the common law of Pennsylvania . . . not Christianity founded on any particular religious tenets; nor Christianity with an established church and tithes and spiritual courts; but Christianity with liberty of conscience to all men." . . .

The establishment of Protestant Christianity was one not

37

only of law but also, and far more importantly, of culture. Protestant Christianity supplied the nation with its "system of values"—to use the modern phrase—and would do so until the 1920's when the cake of Protestant custom seemed most noticeably to begin crumbling.[9]

As we continue to examine the question of law in relation to the founding of the country, we next encounter Sir William Blackstone (1723-1780). William Blackstone was an English jurist who in the 1760s wrote a very famous work called *Commentaries on the Law of England*. By the time the Declaration of Independence was signed, there were probably more copies of his *Commentaries* in America than in Britain. His *Commentaries* shaped the perspective of American law at that time, and when you read them it is very clear exactly upon what that law was based.

To William Blackstone there were only two foundations for law, nature and revelation, and he stated clearly that he was speaking of the "holy Scripture." That was William Blackstone. And up to the recent past not to have been a master of William Blackstone's *Commentaries* would have meant that you would not have graduated from law school.

There were other well-known lawyers who spelled these things out with total clarity. Joseph Story in his 1829 inaugural address as Dane Professor of Law at Harvard University said, "There never has been a period in which Common Law did not recognize Christianity as laying at its foundation."[10]

Concerning John Adams (1735-1826) Terry East-land says:

. . . most people agreed that our law was rooted, as John Adams had said, in a common moral and religious tradition, one that stretched back to the time Moses went up on Mount Sinai. Similarly almost everyone agreed that our liberties were God-given and should be exercised responsibly. There was a distinction between liberty and license.[11]

What we find then as we look back is that the men who founded the United States of America really understood that upon which they were building their concepts of law and the concepts of government. And until the takeover of our government and law by this other entity, the materialistic, humanistic, chance world view, these things remained the base of government and law.

CHAPTER THREE

The Destruction of Faith and Freedom

And now it is all gone!

In most law schools today almost no one studies William Blackstone unless he or she is taking a course in the history of law. We live in a secularized society and in secularized, sociological law. By sociological law we mean law that has no fixed base but law in which a group of people decides what is sociologically good for society at the given moment; and what they arbitrarily decide becomes law. Oliver Wendell Holmes (1841-1935) made totally clear that this was his position.[1] Frederick Moore Vinson (1890-1953), former Chief Justice of the United States Supreme Court, said, "Nothing is more certain in modern society than the principle that there are no absolutes."[2] Those who hold this position themselves call it sociological law.

41

As the new sociological law has moved away from the original base of the Creator giving the "inalienable rights," etc., it has been natural that this sociological law has then also moved away from the Constitution. William Bentley Ball,[3] in his paper entitled "Religious Liberty: The Constitutional Frontier," says:

I propose that secularism militates against religious liberty, and indeed against personal freedoms generally, for two reasons: first, the familiar fact that secularism does not recognize the existence of the "higher law"; second, because, that being so, secularism tends toward decisions based on the pragmatic public policy of the moment and inevitably tends to resist the submitting of those policies to the "higher" criteria of a constitution.

This moving away from the Constitution is not only by court rulings, for example the First Amendment rulings, which are the very reversal of the original purpose of the First Amendment (see pp. 34-35), but in other ways as well. Quoting again from the same paper by William Bentley Ball:

Our problem consists also, as perhaps this paper has well enough indicated, of *more general* constitutional concepts. Let me refer to but two: the unconstitutional delegation of legislative power and *ultra vires.* The first is where the legislature hands over its powers to agents through the conferral of regulatory power unaccompanied by strict standards. The second is where the agents make up powers on their own—assume powers not given them by the legislature. Under the first, the government of laws largely disappears and the government of men largely replaces it. Under the second, agents' personal "homemade" law replaces the law of the elected representatives of the people.

Naturally, this shift from the Judeo-Christian basis for law and the shift away from the restraints of the Constitution automatically militates against religious liberty. Mr. Ball closes his paper:

Fundamentally, in relation to personal liberty, the Constitution was aimed at restraint of the State. Today, in case after case relating to religious liberty, we encounter the bizarre presumption that it is the other way around; that the State is justified in whatever action, and that religion bears a great burden of proof to overcome that presumption.

It is our job, as Christian lawyers, to destroy that presumption at every turn.

As lawyers discuss the changes in law in the United States, often they speak of the influence of the laws passed in relationship to the Mormons and to the laws involved in the reentrance of the southern states into the national government after the Civil War. These indeed must be considered. But they were not the reason for the drastic change in law in our country. The reason was the takeover by the totally other world view which would never have given the form and freedom in government we have had in Northern Europe (including the United States). That is the central factor in the change.

It is parallel to the difference between modern science beginning with Copernicus and Galileo and the materialistic science which took over in the last century. Materialistic thought would never have produced modern science. Modern science was produced on the Christian base. That is, because an intelligent Creator had created the universe we can in some measure understand the universe and there is, therefore, a reason for observation and experimentation to be optimistically pursued.

Then there was a shift into materialistic science *based on a philosophic change* to the materialistic concept of final reality. This shift was based on no addition to the facts known. It was a choice, in faith, to see things that way.[4] No clearer expression of this could be given than Carl Sagan's arrogant statement on public television—made without any scientific proof for the statement—to 140 million viewers: "The cosmos is all that is or ever was or ever will be." He opened the series, *Cosmos*, with this essentially creedal declaration and went on to build every subsequent conclusion upon it.

There is exactly the same parallel in law. The materialistic-energy, chance concept of final reality never would have produced the form and freedom in government we have in this country and in other Reformation countries. But now it has arbitrarily and arrogantly supplanted the historic Judeo-Christian consensus that provided the base for form and freedom in government. The Judeo-Christian consensus gave greater freedoms than the world has ever known, but it also contained the freedoms so that they did not pound society to pieces. The materialistic concept of reality would not have produced the form-freedom balance, and now that it has taken over it cannot maintain the balance. It has destroyed it.

Will Durant and his wife Ariel together wrote *The Story of Civilization.* The Durants received the 1976 Humanist Pioneer Award. In *The Humanist* magazine of February 1977, Will Durant summed up the humanist problem with regard to personal ethics and social order: "Moreover, we shall find it no easy task to mold a natural ethic strong enough to maintain moral restraint and social order without the support of supernatural consolations, hopes, and fears."

Poor Will Durant! It is not just difficult, it is impossible. He should have remembered the quotation he and Ariel Durant gave from the agnostic Renan in their book *The Lessons of History.* According to the Durants, Renan said in 1866: "If Rationalism wishes to govern the world without regard to the religious needs of the soul, the experience of the French Revolution is there to teach us the consequences of such a blunder."[5] And the Durants themselves say in the same context: "There is no significant example in history, before our time, of a society successfully maintaining moral life without the aid of religion."[6]

Along with the decline of the Judeo-Christian consensus we have come to a new definition and connota-

45

tion of "pluralism." Until recently it meant that the Christianity flowing from the Reformation is not now as dominant in the country and in society as it was in the early days of the nation. After about 1848 the great influx of immigrants to the United States meant a sharp increase in viewpoints not shaped by Reformation Christianity. This, of course, is the situation which exists today. Thus as we stand for religious freedom today, we need to realize that this must include a general religious freedom from the control of the state for all religion. It will not mean just freedom for those who are Christians. It is then up to Christians to show that Christianity is the Truth of total reality in the open marketplace of freedom.

This greater mixture in the United States, however, is now used as an excuse for the new meaning and connotation of pluralism. It now is used to mean that all types of situations are spread out before us, and that it really is up to each individual to grab one or the other on the way past, according to the whim of personal preference. What you take is only a matter of personal choice, with one choice as valid as another. Pluralism has come to mean that everything is acceptable. This new concept of pluralism suddenly is everywhere. There is no right or wrong; it is just a matter of your personal preference. On a recent *Sixty Minutes* program on television, for example, the questions of euthanasia of the old and the growing of marijuana as California's largest paying crop were presented this way. One choice is as valid as another. It is just a matter of personal preference. This new definition and connotation of pluralism is presented in many forms, not only in personal ethics, but in society's ethics and in the choices concerning law.

Now I have a question. In these shifts that have come in law, where were the Christian lawyers during the crucial shift from forty years ago to just a few years ago? These shifts have all come, or have mostly come, in the last eighty years, and the great, titanic shifts have come in the last forty years. Within our lifetime the great shifts in law have taken place. Now that this has happened we can say, surely the Christian lawyers should have seen the change taking place and stood on the wall and blown the trumpets loud and clear. A nonlawyer like myself has a right to feel somewhat let down because the Christian lawyers did not blow the trumpets clearly between, let us say, 1940 and 1970.

When I wrote *How Should We Then Live?* from 1974 to 1976 I worked out of a knowledge of secular philosophy. I moved from the results in secular philosophy, to the results in liberal theology, to the results in the arts, and then I turned to the courts, and especially the Supreme Court. I read Oliver Wendell Holmes and others, and I must say, I was totally appalled by what I read. It was an exact parallel to what I had already known so well from my years of study in philosophy, theology, and the other disciplines.

In the book and film series *How Should We Then*

47

Live? I used the Supreme Court abortion case as the clearest illustration of arbitrary sociological law. But it was only the clearest illustration. The law is shot through with this kind of ruling. It is similar to choosing Fletcher's situational ethics and pointing to it as the clearest illustration of how our society now functions with no fixed ethics. This is only the clearest illustration, because in many ways our society functions on unfixed, situational ethics.

The abortion case in law is exactly the same. It is only the clearest case. Law in this country has become situational law, using the term Fletcher used for his ethics. That is, a small group of people decide arbitrarily what, from their viewpoint, is for the good of society at that precise moment and they make it law, binding the whole society by their personal arbitrary decisions.

But of course! What would we expect? These things are the natural, inevitable results of the material-energy, humanistic concept of the final basic reality. From the material-energy, chance concept of final reality, final reality is, and must be by its nature, silent as to values, principles, or any basis for law. There is no way to ascertain "the ought" from "the is."[7] Not only should we have known what this would have produced, but on the basis of this viewpoint of reality, we should have recognized that *there are no other conclusions that this view could produce.* It is a natural result of really believing that the basic reality of all things is merely material-energy, shaped into its present form by impersonal chance.

No, we must say that the Christians in the legal profession did not ring the bell, and we are indeed very, very far down the road toward a totally humanistic culture. At this moment we are in a humanistic culture, but we are happily not in a totally humanistic culture. But what we must realize is that the drift has been all in this direction. If it is not turned around we will move very rapidly into a *totally* humanistic culture.

The law, and especially the courts, is *the vehicle to force* this total humanistic way of thinking upon the entire population. This is what has happened. The abortion law is a perfect example. The Supreme Court abortion ruling invalidated abortion laws in all fifty states, even though it seems clear that in 1973 the majority of Americans were against abortion. It did not matter. The Supreme Court arbitrarily ruled that abortion was legal, and overnight they overthrew the state laws and forced onto American thinking not only that abortion was legal, but that it was ethical. They, as an elite, thus forced their will on the majority, even though their ruling was arbitrary both legally and medically. Thus law and the courts became the vehicle for forcing a totally secular concept on the population.

But I would say for the comfort of the Christian lawyers, it was not only the lawyers that did not blow the trumpet. Certainly the Bible-believing theologians were not very good at blowing trumpets either. In 1893 Dr. Charles A. Briggs had been put out of the Presbyterian ministry for teaching liberal theology. I would repeat that liberal theology is only humanism in theological terms. Then after Dr. Briggs was put out of the Presbyterian ministry there largely followed a tremendously great silence. Until the twenties and the thirties, few, if any, among the Bible-believing theologians blew a loud horn. By that time it was too late as most of the old line denominations had come under the dominance of liberal theology at the two power centers of the bureaucracies and the seminaries. By then voices were raised. But with rare exceptions, by that time it was too late. From then on, the liberal theologians would increasingly side with the secular humanists in matters of life style and the rulings of sociological law.

And those Bible-believing theologians who did see the theological danger seemed totally blind to what was happening in law and in the total culture. Thus the theologians did no better in seeing the shift from one world view to a totally different world view. Nor did Christian educators do any better either. The failed responsibility covers a wide swath. Christian educators, Christian theologians, Christian lawyers— none of them blew loud trumpets until we were a long, long way down the road toward a humanistically based culture.

But, while this may spread the problem of responsibility around, that does not help us today—except to realize that if we are going to do better we must stop being experts in only seeing these things in bits and pieces. We have to understand that it is one total entity opposed to the other total entity. It concerns truth in regard to final and total reality—not just religious reality, but total reality. And our view of final reality—whether it is material-energy, shaped by impersonal chance, or the living God and Creator—will determine our position on every crucial issue we face today. It will determine our views on the value and dignity of people, the base for the kind of life the individual and society lives, the direction law will take, and whether there will be freedom or some form of authoritarian dominance.

CHAPTER FOUR
The Humanist Religion

The humanists have openly told us their views of final reality. The *Humanist Manifesto I* (1933), page 8[1] says

Religious humanists regard the universe as self-existing and not created.

Humanism asserts that the nature of the universe depicted by modern science makes unacceptable any supernatural or cosmic guarantees of human values.

And Carl Sagan indoctrinated millions of unsuspecting viewers with this humanistic final view of reality in the public television show *Cosmos*: "The cosmos is all that is or ever was or ever will be." The humanist view has infiltrated every level of society.

If we are going to join the battle in a way that has any hope of effectiveness—with Christians truly being salt and the light in our culture and our society—then we must do battle on the entire front. We must not finally even battle on the front for freedom, and specifically not only *our* freedom. It must be on the basis of Truth. Not just religious truths, but the Truth of what the final reality is. Is it impersonal material or is it the living God?

The *Humanist Manifestos I and II* both state that humanism is a religion, a faith. [*Manifesto I*: pages 3 and 7; *Manifesto II*: pages 13 and 24.] *Manifesto I*, page 9, very correctly says: "Nothing human is alien to the religious." Christians of all people should have known, taught, and acted on this. Religion touches all of thought and all of life. And these two religions, Christianity and humanism, stand over against each other as totalities.

The *Humanist Manifestos* not only say that humanism is a religion, but the Supreme Court has declared it to be a religion. The 1961 case of *Torcaso* v. *Watkins* specifically defines secular humanism as a religion equivalent to theistic and other nontheistic religions.

On page 19 the *Humanist Manifesto II* says: "It [the State] should not favor any particular religious bodies through the use of public monies. . . ." Ironically, *it is the humanist religion* which the government and courts in the United States favor over all others!

The ruling of the Supreme Court in the *Torcaso* v. *Watkins* case in 1961 is instructive in another way. It shows that within the span of twenty-eight years the Supreme Court turned radically from a Christian memory to the humanistic consensus. In 1933 in the *United States v. MacIntoch* case about conscientious objection, Justice Hughes stated in his dissent:

The essence of religion is belief in a relation to God involving duties superior to those arising from any human relation. . . . One cannot speak of religious liberty, with proper appreciation of its essential and historical significance, without assuming the existence of a belief in supreme allegiance to the will of God.

In 1965 in *United States v. Seeger*, also about conscientious objection, the Court held that the test of religious belief is a "sincere and meaningful belief which occupies in the life of its possessor a place parallel to that filled by the God of those admittedly qualifying for the exemption." This, of course, is a drastic change away from the position of 1933.

The case *Torcaso v. Watkins* in 1961 takes the final step. Here, theistic religions, nontheistic religions, and pure materialistic humanism as a religion are all equated. And the change was complete in twenty-eight years from 1933 to 1961.

We live in a democracy, or republic, in this country which was born out of the Judeo-Christian base. The freedom that this gives is increasingly rare in the world today. We certainly must use this freedom while we still have it. There was a poll done by a secular group a few years ago which looked across the world to determine where there were freedoms today out of the 150 or so nations. Less than twenty-five were rated as today having significant freedom. We still have it. And it is our calling to do something about it and use it in our democracy while we have it.

Most fundamentally, our culture, society, government, and law are in the condition they are in, *not because of a conspiracy, but because the church has forsaken its duty to be the salt of the culture.* It is the church's duty (as well as its privilege) to do now what it should have been doing all the time—to use the freedom we do have to *be* that salt of the culture. If the slide toward authoritarianism is to be reversed we need a committed Christian church that is dedicated to what John W. Whitehead calls "total revolution in the reformative sense."[2]

Some of us may perhaps have some questions about the Moral Majority and some of the things they have said. But I would say one thing we certainly must do is get our information about anything like the Moral Majority not from the secular media, which so largely have the same humanistic perspective as the rest of culture has today. If we are going to make judgments on any such subject we must not get our final judgments uncritically from media that see things from this perspective and see it that way honestly. Most of the media do not have to be dishonest to slide things in their own direction because they see through the spectacles of a finally relativistic set of ethical personal and social standards.

A good example of this lack of objectivity is public television. One of the public television program directors we approached in Washington, D.C., refused to watch the film *Whatever Happened to the Human Race?*, or even to consider it. As soon as she heard of the position it took concerning abortion, she made the excuse, "We can't program anything that presents only one point of view."

At that same time public television was running *Hard Choices*, a program totally slanted in favor of abortion. The Study Guide which accompanied the series *Hard Choices* speaks clearly for the total view of a materialistic final reality:

The vast majority of people believe there is a design or force in the universe; that it works outside the ordinary mechanics of cause and effect; that it is somehow responsible for both the visible and the moral order of the world. Modern biology has undermined this assumption. Even though it is often asserted that science is fully compatible with our Judeo-Christian ethical tradition, in fact it is not. . . .

To be sure, even in antiquity, the mechanistic view of life—that chance *was* responsible for the shape of the world—had a few adherents. But belief in overarching order was dominant; it can be seen as easily in such scientists as Newton, Harvey, and Einstein as in the theologians Augustine, Luther, and Tillich. But beginning with Darwin, biology has undermined that tradition. Darwin in effect asserted that all living organisms had been created by a combination of chance and necessity—natural selection.

57

In the twentieth century, this view of life has been rein-
forced by a whole series of discoveries. . . .

Mind is the only remaining frontier, but it would be
shortsighted to doubt that it can, one day, be duplicated in
the form of thinking robots or analyzed in terms of the
chemistry and electricity of the brain.

The extreme mechanistic view of life, which every new
discovery in biology tends to confirm, has certain implications. First, God has no role in the physical world. . . .

Second, except for the laws of probability and cause and
effect, there is no organizing principle in the world, and no
purpose. Thus, there are no moral or ethical laws that
belong to the nature of things, no absolute guiding principles for human society. . . .

The mechanistic view of life has perhaps only one tangi-
ble implication for ethics: we should feel freer to adapt our
morality to new social situations. But we are already fairly
adept at that. . . . As a result, ethical choices are likely to
become more difficult, not because people are less moral
but because they will be unable to justify their choices with
fairy tales.[3]

Here is public tax money being used not only in favor
of abortion but to teach the whole view of a materialistic, mechanistic universe, shaped only by chance, with
no final purpose and with morals (and law) purely a
matter of social choice. The Judeo-Christian view is
pushed into the category of "fairy tales."

How much this sounds like the *Humanist Manifesto
II*, page 13, which said:

As in 1933 [the date of the *Humanist Manifesto I*] humanists still believe that traditional theism, especially faith in the prayer-hearing God, assumed to love and care for persons, to hear and understand their prayers, and to be able to do something about them, is an unproved and outmoded faith. Salvationism, based on mere affirmation, still appears as harmful, diverting people with false hopes of heaven hereafter. Reasonable minds look to other means for survival.

Once again we are reminded of public television's airing of *Cosmos* by Carl Sagan which teaches as dogma that the impersonal cosmos is all there is or ever was or ever will be.

In this setting we must indeed not expect objectivity from the media.

Even the most respected commentators are affected. On the eve of Walter Cronkite's retirement as anchorman on the CBS Evening News he gave an interview in Monte Carlo to Jeffrey Robinson of the *International Herald Tribune*, featured in the February 18, 1981 issue. In it, Walter Cronkite questions whether, with television, democracy is any longer a suitable political philosophy—whether we can still be sure that democracy can work. Reporting on the interview the *Tribune* observes:

He [Cronkite] seriously suggests that under the high technology circumstances of today, there might be some questions as to whether or not democracy is a suitable political philosophy.

The article continues, quoting Cronkite directly:

"I'm not saying that the answer should immediately come down on the side of no. I support democracy. I'm simply saying that there is a question. I think there is a hell of a lot of explaining to be done before we can be sure that democracy can work."

The media and especially television have indeed changed the *perception* of not only current events, but also of the political process. We must realize that things can easily be presented on television so that the *perception* of a thing may be quite different from fact itself. Television not only reports political happenings, it enters actively into the political process. That is, either because of bias or for a good story, television so reports the political process that it influences and becomes a crucial part of the political process itself. A good example was Walter Cronkite's part in orchestrating the Gerald Ford candidacy for Vice-President at the 1980 Republican Convention.

We must realize that the communications media function much like the unelected federal bureaucracy. They are so powerful that they act as if they were the fourth branch of government in the United States. Charles Peters, editor-in-chief of *The Washington Monthly*, in his book *How Washington Really Works*,[4] writes that the media, instead of exposing the "make believe" of the federal government, are "part of the show."

Television (and the communications media in general) thus are not only reporting news, but making it. Their ability to change our *perception* of any event raises serious questions concerning the democratic processes.

The solution is not the one Cronkite gives in his interview—perhaps changing to a political philosophy different from democracy. The solution is to limit somehow television's power to use its bias in "the editorial" reporting of events,[5] and most specifically to keep it from shaping the political process.

In the midst of all this Christians must certainly not uncritically accept what they read, and especially what they see on television, as objective. This is especially the case when the subject under consideration is one we know to be different from that which their world view normally causes them to champion.

Returning to the Moral Majority, we must realize that regardless of whether we think the Moral Majority has always said the right things or whether we do not, or whether we think they have made some mistakes or whether we do not, they have certainly done one thing right: they have used the freedom we still have in the political arena to stand against the other total entity. They have carried the fact that law is king, law is above the lawmakers, and God is above the law into this area of life where it always should have been. And this is a part of true spirituality.

The Moral Majority has drawn a line between the one total view of reality and the other total view of reality and the results this brings forth in government and law. And if you personally do not like some of the details of what they have done, do it better. But you must understand that all Christians have got to do the same kind of thing or you are simply not showing the Lordship of Christ in the totality of life.

CHAPTER FIVE
Revival, Revolution, and Reform

As we turn to the evangelical leadership of this country in the last decades, unhappily, we must come to the conclusion that often it has not been much help. It has shown the mark of a platonic, overly spiritualized Christianity all too often. Spirituality to the evangelical leadership often has not included the Lordship of Christ over the whole spectrum of life. Spirituality has often been shut up to a very narrow area. And also very often, among many evangelicals, including evangelical leaders, it seems that the final end is to protect their own projects. I am not saying all, by any means, but all too often that has been the case. I am again asking the question, why have we let ourselves go so far down the road? And this is certainly one of the answers.

Now you must remember, this is a rather new phe-

nomenon. The old revivals are spoken about so warm-
ly by the evangelical leadership. Yet they seem to have
forgotten what those revivals were. Yes, the old revivals in Great Britain, in Scandinavia, and so on, and
the old revivals in this country did call, without any
question and with tremendous clarity, for personal
salvation. But they also called for a resulting social
action. Read the history of the old revivals. Every
single one of them did this, and there can be no greater example than the great revivals of John Wesley
(1703-1791) and George Whitefield (1714-1770).

Concerning Wesley, Howard A. Snyder says:

Migration to the cities had produced a new class of urban
poor in Wesley's day. The Industrial Revolution was in full
swing, fired by coal. When Wesley preached to the Kings-
wood colliers he was touching those most cruelly victimized
by industrialization. Yet his response among the coal miners was phenomenal, and Wesley worked tirelessly for their
spiritual and material welfare. Among other things, he
opened free dispensaries, set up a kind of credit union, and
established schools and orphanages. His ministry branched
out to include lead miners, iron smelters, brass and copper
workers, quarrymen, shipyard workers, farm laborers, pris-
oners and women industrial workers.

To all these people—the victims of society—Wesley
offered the Good News of Jesus Christ. But he did more. He
formed them into close-knit fellowships where they could
be shepherded and where leaders could be developed, and
he worked to reform the conditions under which they lived.
His efforts went beyond welfare to include creative eco-

nomic alternatives. Through his pointed and prolific writings he agitated for major reforms. He was convinced that "the making an open stand against all the ungodliness and unrighteousness which overspreads our land as a flood, is one of the noblest ways of confessing Christ in the face of His enemies."[1]

The Wesley and Whitefield revivals were tremendous in calling for individual salvation, and thousands upon thousands were saved. Yet even secular historians acknowledge that it was the social results coming out of the Wesley revival that saved England from its own form of the French Revolution. If it had not been for the Wesley revival and its social results, England would almost certainly have had its own "French Revolution." We should sound the names of some of our Christian predecessors with a cry of pride and thankfulness to God: Lord Shaftesbury (1801-1855), who dared to stand for justice for the poor in the midst of the Industrial Revolution; William Wilberforce (1759-1833), who was the greatest single personal force in changing England from a slave-owning country to a country that turned away legally and totally from slavery long before the United States did. These men did not do these things incidentally, but because they saw it as a part of the Christian good news. God used those involved in the revivals to bring forth the results not only of individual salvation, but also social action.

Jeremy Rifkin, whom some of you will know as a

leading counter-culture figure of the sixties, in 1980 wrote *Entropy*.[2] In this book he shows that he understands, far better than the evangelical leadership often has, that the old revivals resulted in social action. He quotes *Pollution and the Death of Man—The Christian View of Ecology*[3] at length in the chapter he calls "The Second Reformation," pointing out that there is a different possibility for a Christian answer in regard to ecology. He really understands something, though not as a Christian (for he continues in his pantheistic framework). But he really comprehends that in the days of the revivals and today there are Christian answers for social action and answers in areas such as ecology. Christianity does have answers.

Now when we come nearer to home, Wheaton College stands out as a great name in evangelical circles. In the old days Oberlin College was known as a great Bible-believing college. But it is no longer; it is liberal. Happily Wheaton is not. But what most people do not realize is that Jonathan Blanchard (1811-1892), who was the founder and president of Wheaton College, and Charles Finney (1792-1875), who was the president of Oberlin College, were tremendously interested in the question of social action concerning slavery. They were two great voices in America calling out for social action, and both of them said something very firmly: *If a law is wrong, you must disobey it.* Both of them call, when it is necessary, for civil disobedience.

Finney in his book *Systematic Theology* on page 158

has a heading: "I propose now to make several remarks respecting forms of government, the right and duty of revolution." Do note his phrase "The right and duty of revolution." On page 162 he says: "There can scarcely be conceived a more abominable and fiendish maxim than 'our country right or wrong.' " He then goes on to stress that not everything the government does is to be supported, and he includes the Mexican War and slavery. On page 157 he says: "Arbitrary legislation can never be really obligatory."[4]

And we must not forget that Jonathan Kaufman was right when he wrote in the *Wall Street Journal*: ". . . [it was the] Great Religious Awakening two and one half centuries ago that helped sow the seeds of the American Revolution. . . ."[5]

Our evangelical leadership seems to have forgotten its heritage. When the book and film series *Whatever Happened to the Human Race?* came out we observed something very instructive. The call for a public stand against abortion, infanticide, euthanasia, and against the general eradication of the unique dignity and worth of all human beings was not widely accepted at first. Many of the evangelical leadership either were totally silent about abortion, or qualified what they did say about abortion to such an extent that they really said nothing, or less than nothing, as far as the battle for human life was concerned.

The seminars for *Whatever Happened to the Human Race?* were marvelous seminars certainly. My wife and

67

I both agree we have never seen people go out of seminars or meetings so committed to action. People went out from those seminars and there was a change. Prior to that, to our shame, across the United States and Great Britain as well, there were very, very few evangelicals involved in the movement against abortion. We had left it to the Roman Catholics to such an extent that the battle for human life was being lost by the simple tactic of its being called "a Roman Catholic issue." After this project, happily, there were more evangelicals who saw the importance of the issue of human life and bringing the Lordship of Christ concerning law into this very important area.

But often the seminars were not well attended. We found that it was often because much of the evangelical leadership did not want to become involved. With some it was the prison of their platonic spirituality, and this, of course, makes them incapable of engaging in any such warfare. Franky Schaeffer V writes in *Addicted to Mediocrity*:

Either God is the Creator of the whole man, the whole universe, and all of reality and existence, or he is the Creator of none of it. If God is only the Creator of some divided platonic existence which leads to a tension between the body and the soul, the real world and the spiritual world, if God is only the Creator of some spiritual little experiential "praise the Lord" reality, then he is not much of a God. Indeed, he is not I AM at all. If our Christian lives are allowed to become something spiritual

68

and religious as opposed to something real, daily applicable, understandable, beautiful, verifiable, balanced, sensible, and above all united, whole, if indeed our Christianity is allowed to become this waffling spiritual goo that nineteenth-century platonic Christianity became, then Christianity as truth disappears and instead we only have a system of vague experiential religious platitudes in its place.[6]

With some it was their desire not to have their own projects disturbed. There were cases where some not only did not urge people to come, but where other meetings were planned which hindered people from coming. A very unhappy thing. No, the Christian lawyers, theologians, and educators, indeed, much of the evangelical establishment, certainly have not been in there blowing the trumpet loud and clear.

We must understand that the question of the dignity of human life is not something on the periphery of Judeo-Christian thinking, but almost in the center of it (though not *the* center because the center is the existence of God Himself). But the dignity of human life is unbreakably linked to the existence of the personal-infinite God. It is because there is a personal-infinite God who has made men and women in His own image that they have a unique dignity of life as human beings. Human life then is filled with dignity, and the state and humanistically oriented law have no right and no authority to take human life arbitrarily in the way that it is being taken.

We must see then that indeed the cry has not been given. We must see that here, on such a central issue as abortion, the true nature of the problem was not understood: Christians failed to see that abortion was really a symptom of the much larger problem and not just one bit and piece. And beyond this as the material-energy-chance humanistic world view takes over increasingly in our country, the view concerning the intrinsic value of human life will grow less and less, and the concept of compassion for which the country is in some sense known will be further gone.

A girl who has been working with the Somalian refugees has just been in our home and told us their story and shown us their pictures. One million—and especially little children—in agony, pain, and suffering! Can we help but cry? But forget it! In the United States we now kill by painful methods one and a half times that many each year by abortion. In Somalia it is war. But we kill in cold blood. The compassion our country has been known somewhat for is being undermined. And it is not only the babies who are being killed; it is humanness which the humanist world view is beating to death.

The people in the United States have lived under the Judeo-Christian consensus for so long that now we take it for granted. We seem to forget how completely unique what we have had is a result of the gospel. The gospel indeed is, "accept Christ, the Messiah, as Savior and have your guilt removed on the basis of His death." But the good news includes many resulting blessings. We have forgotten why we have a high view of life, and why we have a positive balance between form and freedom in government, and the fact that we have such tremendous freedoms without these freedoms leading to chaos. Most of all, we have forgotten that none of these is natural in the world. They are unique, based on the fact that the consensus was the biblical consensus. And these things will be even further lost if this other total view, the materialistic view, takes over more thoroughly. We can be certain that what we so carelessly take for granted will be lost.

CHAPTER SIX
An Open Window

What is ahead of us? I would suggest that we must
have *Two Tracks* in mind.

The *First Track* is the fact of the conservative swing
in the United States in the 1980 election. With this
there is at this moment a unique window open in the
United States. It is unique because it is a long, long
time since that window has been open as it is now.
And let us hope that the window stays open, and not
on just one issue, even one as important as human
life—though certainly every Christian ought to be
praying and working to nullify the abominable abortion law. But as we work and pray, we should have in
mind not only this important issue as though it stood
alone. Rather, we should be struggling and praying
that this whole other total entity—the material-
energy, chance world view—can be rolled back with

all its results across all of life. I work, I pray that indeed the window does stay open. I hope that will be the case.

Now the window is open and we must take advantage of it in every way we can as citizens, as Christian citizens of the democracy in which we still have freedom. We must try to roll back the other total entity. It will not be easy to roll it back because those who hold the other total world view of reality have no intention that it will be rolled back. Those who hold this view are deeply entrenched, they have had their own way without opposition for a long time, and they will use every means to see that the momentum they have achieved, and the results they have brought forth in all fields, will be retained and enlarged.

For example, all you have to do is to consider the way the media treated Dr. C. Everett Koop. Dr. Koop is one of the foremost pediatric surgeons in the United States, and among other honors, he was given the highest honor of the French government for his pioneering work in pediatric surgery. But when he was nominated for the position of Surgeon General, he was attacked by the secular media with total disregard for objective reporting—and with total disregard for his brilliant humanitarian record as a surgeon. Those in the media holding the humanist world view could not tolerate Dr. Koop's voice to be heard—they could not tolerate his articulate defense of the sanctity of human life to be expressed.

74

We must understand that there is going to be a battle every step of the way. They are determined that what they have gained will not be rolled back. But it is our task to use the open window to try to change that direction at this very late hour. And we must press on, hoping, praying, and working that indeed the window can stay open and the total entity will be pressed back rather than the whole thing ending only in words.

Some of us, however, who have some position of leadership, must unhappily be thinking of the possible *Second Track*.

The *Second Track* is, What happens in this country if the window does not stay open? What then?

Thinking this way does not mean that we stop doing all we can to keep the window open. Nevertheless some people must be thinking about what to do if the window closes. And though we hope it stays open, what happens if it does not?

Now let's ask ourselves where we are in the sociological atmosphere of our country. Think of the counter-culture people out of the sixties. By the end of the sixties they had given up their hope of an ideological solution on the basis of drugs or on the basis of Marcuse's New Left. That is, by the end of the sixties they had given up their two optimistic, ideological hopes.

As we consider those who came out of the sixties and the seventies we see there are not many anarchists around us in the United States. In Europe, however, there are a growing number of young anarchists—in West Germany, especially West Berlin, Holland, Great Britain, and even Switzerland. These anarchists are there. They have a cry, "No power to nobody!" They paint a large A on the walls of beautiful cathedrals and beautiful old churches and government buildings. Anarchists! They are nihilists. I saw a graffito on the wall of a government building in Lausanne a few nights ago which read: "The State is the enemy. The Church is the collaborator." What they practice in their lives is exactly what the words of punk rock say. Most people do not listen to the words of punk rock, even if they listen to the music. The words of punk rock speak of nihilism, hopelessness, the meaninglessness of life, anarchy. This group in Europe is now living that way and in practice stands against the total society.

But that has not happened in the United States. In the seventies the counter-culture young people who had given up the hope of an *ideological solution* of drugs and of Marcuse's New Left began to join the system in order to get their part of the affluence and thus be able to live their own lifestyle. That is what we find in the seventies and the beginning of the eighties. They may continue to use drugs but no longer as an ideological solution. If they use drugs it is now rather as the traditional use of drugs, for personal escape.

Now I want to add something to that. In the Nixon era we heard a lot about the Silent Majority, but most people did not realize that there were two parts to that Silent Majority among the older people. There was the *majority* of the Silent Majority and there was the *minority* of the Silent Majority.

The *majority* of the Silent Majority were those who had only two bankrupt values—personal peace and affluence. Personal peace means just to be let alone, not to be troubled by the troubles of other people, whether across the world or across the city. Affluence means an overwhelming and ever-increasing prosperity—a life made up of things and more things—a success judged by an ever-higher level of material abundance.

On the other hand, the *minority* of the Silent Majority were those who were standing on some kind of principle, and often with at least a memory of Christianity even if they were not individually Christians.

We must realize that if you take the join-the-system young people and the majority of the Silent Majority, though they may have very different lifestyles, they support each other completely sociologically. They are in exactly the same place. In this respect, we must remember that although there are tremendous discrepancies between conservatives and liberals in the political arena, if they are both operating on a humanistic base there will really be no final difference between them. As Christians we must stand absolutely and totally opposed to the whole humanist system, *whether*

77

it is controlled by conservative or liberal elements. Thus Christians must not become officially aligned with either group just on the basis of the name it uses.

Terry Eastland in *Commentary* says:

It is the style nowadays not only among the college-educated but also among many blue-collar workers to be economically conservative but socially and morally liberal. This, translated, means balance the budget but decriminalize marijuana and cocaine and let us have abortion on demand. If the liberalism of the sixties has a definite legacy, it is found in the far more liberalized and hedonistic lives many Americans, including many older Americans, and indeed many political conservatives, now lead.[1]

What percentage in the 1980 election voted out of principle and what percentage voted for a change of some sort in order to increase their own affluence? George F. Will is a columnist for 360 newspapers, including the *Washington Post,* and is a contributing editor for *Newsweek.* In a February 16, 1981, article entitled "Rhetoric and Reality" in the *International Herald Tribune,* he wrote: "In 1980, the electorate's mandate probably was about 20 percent for conservatism and 80 percent for improved economic numbers, no matter how produced." Notice the important phrase: "no matter how produced."

Long before I read that quote I said that was what had happened. I would not dare give such exact percentages, but I think what George Will is stating is exactly the case. And if the improved economic numbers are not forthcoming, then what? With the two sociological groups of the join-the-system young people and the affluence-centered older ones supporting each other, do you think the window that is open will stay open?

With the window that is open we must beware of letting a foolish triumphalism cause us to think that all is now won and certain. We hear: "There is a new wind blowing." True, but often those who say this, or something like it, then forget that this does not mean the new wind will automatically keep blowing. It does not mean we can return to the practice of false views of spirituality. And it does not mean we can withdraw from a struggle for continued reformation, even if it is at great cost to us personally and to our favorite projects.

And if the window does close, if people do not get their "economic numbers no matter how produced," I do not think there will be a return to the old liberalism of the last fifty years. Rather, my guess is that there will be some form of an elite authoritarianism just as I suggested at the conclusion of How Should We Then Live?[2]

All that would be needed in much of the Western world is even an illusion of what George Will calls "improved economic numbers" to accept some form of an elite to give at least the illusion of these numbers. And as I said in How Should We Then Live? this will be especially so if it is brought in under the guise of constitutionality as it was under Caesar Augustus in the Roman Empire. If it could be brought in in that way I think there would be hardly a ripple.

What form of elite might take over? A number of thinkers have set forth their predictions. John Kenneth Galbraith (1908-   ) has suggested an elite composed of intellectuals (especially from the academic and scientific world) plus government. Daniel Bell (1919-   ), professor of sociology at Harvard University, saw an elite composed of select intellectuals made up of those who control the use of the technological explosion, a technocratic elite. Speaking more recently, Gerald Holton (1922-   ), Mallinckrodt Professor of physics and professor of the history of science at Harvard University, seems to agree with Bell. *The Chronicle of Higher Education*, May 18, 1981, quotes Holton in an article entitled, "Where is Science Taking Us? Gerald Holton Maps the Possible Routes."

Therein lies the problem. More and more frequently, major decisions that profoundly affect our daily lives have a large scientific or technological content, he says. "By a recent estimate, nearly half the bills before the U.S. Congress have a substantial science-technology component," he says, and "some two-thirds of the District of Columbia Circuit Court's case load now involves review of action by federal administrative agencies; and more and more of such cases relate to matters on the frontiers of technology.

"If the layman cannot participate in decision making, he will have to turn himself over, essentially blind, to a

An Open Window

hermetic elite," Mr. Holton said in the interview last week. Then, he continued, the fundamental question becomes, "Are we still capable of self-government and therefore of freedom?

"Margaret Mead wrote in a 1959 issue of *Daedalus* about scientists elevated to the status of priests," Mr. Holton said.

"Now there is a name for this elevation, when you are in the hands of—one hopes—a benevolent elite, when you have no control over your political decisions. From the point of view of John Locke, the name for this is slavery."

For myself I think we should not rule out the courts, and especially the Supreme Court, as being such an elite for these reasons:

1. They are already ruling on the basis of sociological, arbitrary law.
2. They are *making* much law, as well as ruling on law.
3. They dominate the two other parts of government.

They rule on what the other two branches of government can and cannot do, and they usually go unchallenged. It has been said that in the last couple of years the Supreme Court has tended to defer to the other two branches of government. However, while one could hope this will set a trend toward self-restraint away from an "Imperial Court," the figures suggest otherwise. In the first 195 years of the existence of the United States the Supreme Court voided only ninety-one acts of Congress—that is, considerably less than one every two years. In the last ten years it has voided fifteen acts of Congress—that is, an aver-

81

age of one and a half acts of Congress have been voided each year.

At the same time I would stress the fact that the main point is not trying to choose at this moment what the elite might be. Instead we must realize the possibility of such an elite if the masses do not get their "economic numbers." As I write this there are strikes in Britain—partially, at least, because of the price of rectifying fifty or so years of flagrant economic spending. The United States has also had its fifty years of spending, and this presents a painful problem. Indeed, the political price for solving the problem may be too high to make any solution possible.

I hope the window does not close. I hope those with a humanistic world view who have increasingly controlled our culture for the last twenty, thirty, forty years, something like this, cannot close the open window with all their efforts. But if they do, if they take over with increased power and control, will we be so foolish as to think that religion and the religious institutions will not be even further affected than they have been so far? I wonder how many of us are aware of the cases that the churches have faced in the last ten years in various places. The things that have been brought into courts of law should make our hair stand on end. Do you think that in such a case as I have portrayed (and may it not happen!) that the Christians and the Christian institutions will not be even further affected?

Robert L. Toms, an attorney-at-law, lists the issues pending this year and which are up for final adjudication during the coming decade before the United States' courts, administrative bodies, executive departments, and legislatures:

1. Is a minister of the gospel liable for malpractice to a counselee for using spiritual guidance rather than psychological or medical techniques?

2. Can a Christian residence house in a college have the same standing as a fraternity and sorority house for purposes of off-campus residency rules?

3. Can Christian high school students assemble on the public school campus for religious discussion?

4. Can Christian teachers in public schools meet before class for prayer?

5. Can Christian college students meet in groups on the state university campus?

6. Can HEW require a Bible college to admit drug addicts and alcoholics as "handicapped persons"?

7. Can a church build a religious school or a day-care center in an area zoned residential?

8. Can parents who send their children to religious schools not approved by a state board of education be prosecuted under the truancy laws?

9. Is an independent, wholly religious school entitled to an exemption from unemployment taxes as are church-owned schools?

10. Will the State enforce antiemployment discrimination laws against a church which in accordance with its stated religious beliefs fires a practicing homosexual staff member?

11. Can seminary trustees refuse to graduate a practicing homosexual?

12. Can a city continue its forty-year practice of having a nativity scene in front of the city hall?

13. Can zoning laws be used to prevent small group Bible studies from meeting in homes?

14. Can a court decide which doctrinal group in a church split gets the sanctuary?

15. Must a religious school accept as a teacher an otherwise qualified practicing homosexual?

16. Can a church be fined by a court for exuberant noise in worship?

17. Can a state department of health close a church-run juvenile home for policies that include spanking?

18. Can religious solicitation in public places be confined to official booths?

19. Is an unborn fetus a "person" and entitled to Constitutional protection?

20. Can The Ten Commandments be posted in a public classroom?

21. Can students in public education have a period of silent meditation and prayer?

22. Can Christmas carols be sung in the public schools?

23. Must an employee who believes he should worship on Saturday be permitted a work holiday on that day in order to worship?

24. Can the graduation ceremony of a public high school be held in a church?

25. Can a State official seize a church on allegations of misconduct by dissident members and run the church through a court-appointed receiver?

26. Can the State set minimum standards for private religious school curricula?

27. Is religious tax exemption a right or privilege, and, if it is a privilege, are the exemptions an unwarranted support of religion by the State?

28. Should churches be taxed like any other part of society?

29. Can Federal labor laws be used to enforce collective bargaining rights and unionization in religious enterprises?

30. Can the State require a license before a religious ministry may solicit funds for its work?

31. Are hospitals, schools, counseling groups, halfway houses, famine-relief organizations, youth organizations,

homes for unwed mothers, orphanages, etc., run with religious motivations or are they secular and subject to all controls secular organizations are subject to?[3]

He further says:

. . . two U.S. trial courts have recently ruled that a group of college students who wish to discuss religion could not meet in the context of a public state university, that religious speech must go on elsewhere since it might "establish religion" on the campus. . . . The State must screen out religious speech from the otherwise free speech practiced on a university campus.[4]

We might differ as to what the ruling should be in some of these cases, but that does not change the weight of the whole. It should be said that it is not only Protestants who are facing the implications of the above list, but Roman Catholics and Jews as well.

And for Christians who are in the habit of drifting complacently, a case presently before the courts should be a loud-sounding alarm bell. As I write, Samuel E. Ericsson, an attorney-at-law, is defending Grace Community Church, the largest Protestant church in Los Angeles County, in a clergyman malpractice suit. This suit was brought by parents because the pastors of that church cared for their son (who had later committed suicide) instead of turning him over to professional psychiatric and psychological care.[5]

Obviously if the church lost this case, all religions would be greatly affected. In fact, anyone who tried to help someone with questions or fears could be sued if he or she did not fall under the category of professional psychiatric and psychological competence. And to make matters more complicated, no one has thought how to set standards acceptably for professional psychiatric and psychological competence!

Samuel Ericsson has put the case in the proper perspective when in a letter to me dated May 1, 1981, he wrote: "I believe that clergyman malpractice, or more accurately spiritual counseling malpractice, is going to present the secular courts with a head-on clash between the two competing world views, secularism and Christianity."

Should not all of us be thinking what to do about it if the window does shut? The Christian theologians, the educators, the lawyers, the evangelical leadership, have not had a very good record in the past of seeing things as a whole. That is, they have not seen the contrast between the consensus which is based on there being a Law Giver and what that naturally brings forth, and the totally different material-energy, chance world view of reality and what that naturally brings forth. Now if we have not run very well in the past with the footmen when it has been so very easy, I wonder what is going to happen to us if we have to run with the horsemen? What will protect us from what is happening in most of the world today? Have we run with the footmen? Very, very poorly. What happens if we must run with the horsemen?

CHAPTER SEVEN
The Limits of Civil Obedience

The Founding Fathers and those in the thirteen states understood what they were building upon. We have reached a place today which is violently opposed to what the Founding Fathers of this country and those in the thirteen individual states had in mind when they came together and formed the union.

It is time to think to *the bottom line* as our forefathers did. What was *the bottom line* that our forefathers thought to that made it possible for them to act as they did?

First, what is the final relationship to the state on the part of anyone whose base is the existence of God? How would you answer that question?

You must understand that those in our present material-energy, chance oriented generation have *no reason* to obey the state except that the state has the

89

guns and has the patronage. That is the only reason they have for obeying the state. A material-energy, chance orientation gives no base, no reason, except force and patronage, as to why citizens should obey the state.

The Christian, the God-fearing person, is not like that. The Bible tells us that God has commanded us to obey the state.

But now a second question follows very quickly. Has God set up an authority in the state that is autonomous from Himself? Are we to obey the state no matter what? Are we? In this one area is indeed Man the measure of all things? And I would answer, not at all, not at all.

When Jesus says in Matthew 22:21: "Give to Caesar what is Caesar's, and to God what is God's," it is not:

GOD and CAESAR

It was, is, and it always will be:

GOD
and
CAESAR

The civil government, as all of life, stands under the Law of God. In this fallen world God has given us certain offices to protect us from the chaos which is the natural result of that fallenness. But when *any office* commands that which is contrary to the Word of God, those who hold that office abrogate their authority and they are not to be obeyed. And that includes the state.

Romans 13:1-4 says

Everyone must submit himself to the governing authorities, for there is no authority except that which God has established. The authorities that exist have been established by God. Consequently, he who rebels against the authority is rebelling against what God has instituted, and those who do so will bring judgment on themselves. For rulers hold no terror for those who do right, but for those who do wrong. Do you want to be free from fear of the one in authority? Then do what is right and he will commend you. For he is God's servant to do you good. But if you do wrong, be afraid, for he does not bear the sword for nothing. He is God's servant, an agent of wrath to bring punishment on the wrongdoer.

God has ordained the state as a *delegated* authority; it is not autonomous. The state is to be an agent of justice, to restrain evil by punishing the wrongdoer, and to protect the good in society. When it does the reverse, *it has no proper authority*. It is then a usurped authority and as such it becomes lawless and is tyranny.

In 1 Peter 2:13-17 we read:

Submit yourselves for the Lord's sake to every authority instituted among men: whether to the king, as the supreme authority, or to governors, who are sent by him to punish those who do wrong and to commend those who do right. For it is God's will that by doing good you should silence the ignorant talk of foolish men. Live as free men, but do not use your freedom as a cover-up for evil; live as servants of God. Show proper respect to everyone: Love the brotherhood of believers, fear God, honor the king.

Peter says here that civil authority is to be honored and that God is to be feared. The state, as he defines it, is to punish those who do wrong and commend those who do right. If this is not so, then the whole structure falls apart. Clearly, the state is to be a ministry of justice. This is the legitimate function of the state, and in this structure Christians are to obey the state as a matter of "conscience" (Romans 13:5).

But what is to be done when the state does that which violates its legitimate function? The early Christians died because they would not obey the state in a civil matter. People often say to us that the early church did not show any civil disobedience. They do not know church history. Why were the Christians in the Roman Empire thrown to the lions? From the Christian's viewpoint it was for a religious reason. But from the viewpoint of the Roman State they were in civil disobedience, they were civil rebels. The Roman State did not care what anybody believed religiously; you could believe anything, or you could be an atheist. But you had to worship Caesar as a sign of your loyalty to the state. The Christians said they would not worship Caesar, anybody, or anything, but the living God. Thus to the Roman Empire they were rebels, and it was civil disobedience. That is why they were thrown to the lions.

Francis Legge in volume one of his book *Forerunners and Rivals of Christianity from 330 B.C. to A.D. 330* writes: "The officials of the Roman Empire in times of persecution sought to force the Christians to sacrifice, not to any heathen gods, but to the Genius of the Emperor and the Fortune of the City of Rome; and at all times the Christians' refusal was looked upon not as a religious but as a political offense."[1]

The bottom line is that at a certain point there is not only the right, but the duty, to disobey the state.

Through the ages Christians have taken the same position as did the early church in disobeying the state when it commanded what was contrary to God's Law. William Tyndale (c. 1490-1536), the English translator of the Bible, advocated the supreme authority of the Scripture over and against the state and the church. Government authorities continually sought to capture him, but Tyndale was successful in evading them for years. Tyndale was eventually condemned as a heretic, tried and executed on October 6, 1536. John Bunyan (1628-1688) was found guilty of breaking the king's law. Arrested three times for preaching without a state license and for failing to attend the Church of England, he spent twelve years in an English jail. He wrote many works from this jail cell, including *Pilgrim's Progress*.

In almost every place where the Reformation had success there was some form of civil disobedience or armed rebellion:

Netherlands: Catholic Spain had isolated the non-Catholic population both politically and geographically. Thus the Protestants concentrated in what is now Holland which became the last holdout against the Spanish power. The leaders of the revolt established Protestantism as the dominant religious form of the country. The turning point was the battle for Leyden in 1574. The Dutch Protestants fought a very hard and costly battle. When they finally won, the door was open not only for the subsequent political entity of Holland, but also for the successful Dutch Reformation with all its cultural as well as religious results.

Sweden: In 1527 the Vasa family broke away from Denmark as an act of rebellion and established Sweden as a Lutheran country. Later, in 1630, it was the Swedish king, Gustavus Adolphus, a sincere champion of Lutheranism, who marched his army out of Sweden and into Germany against the Emperor to protect Protestant Germany with his force of arms.

Denmark: In 1536 the Protestant party of nobles overthrew the Danish dynasty—an act of "civil disobedience" with accompanying strife. They then set up a new government and a new dynasty and established Lutheranism in the country.

Germany: Luther was protected by the Duke of Saxony against the political and military power of the Emperor. After many wars in which the Duke of Saxony and other German nobles kept the Emperor at bay, the Peace of Augsburg was signed in 1555. In this it was established that the ruler's religion would determine the religion of his geographical location. Thus the German Reformation won its right to exist. Later, with the rise of the Roman Catholic Counter-Reformation, the Thirty Years War was fought, and out of this came the Peace of Westphalia in 1648 which ratified the 1555 Peace of Augsburg. By this, German Protestantism was protected from the reprisals of the Counter-Reformation.

Switzerland: Bern established reform and Protestantism between 1523 and 1525 by Communal vote. Yet for what is now the Canton of Vaud (where I live), it was Protestant Bern's military control of this area at that time which gave William Farel his opportunity to preach the gospel in Aigle and Ollon, leading to reformation in French-speaking Switzerland.

Geneva: This area became Protestant by vote of the Common Council in 1533-1534. Calvin came to Geneva in 1536. There was no open war, but the Reformation was established despite the constant threat of war by the House of Savoy.

Because John Knox of Scotland is such a clear example I will give more detail concerning him.[2] Knox was ordained to the priesthood in 1536 (the year William Tyndale was executed) after studying at St. Andrews University near Edinburgh where Samuel Rutherford later was Rector. Knox was also a lawyer and a bodyguard to the fiery evangelist George Wishart.

Shortly thereafter, Knox accepted a call to the ministry and began attacking the Roman Catholic Church. This was extremely dangerous since the Roman Catholic Church exerted a dominant influence over the Scottish State. Knox was prevented from preaching on Sundays (the dates were conveniently filled by priests). Knox held services on weekdays during which he refuted what was said by others on Sundays. So successful were his efforts that a majority of those in Edinburgh made an open profession of the Protestant faith by participating in the Lord's Supper as administered by Knox.

On June 30, 1547, Knox, along with others, was captured by French forces in the war with England. Disaster that this was, it was better than what would have happened if the Scottish government had apprehended him. Most likely, he would have been burned at the stake.

After almost two years as a galley slave, Knox gained his liberty. He landed as a refugee in England in 1549 and resumed preaching. He was so effective that Protestant families in Scotland, hearing of his ministry, crossed the border illegally and resettled in Berwick, England, so as to be near him.

Knox is rightly thought of as a radical reformer. There is, however, an important distinction to keep in mind concerning him. Throughout his ministry, Knox appealed for moderation and compromise whenever truly fundamental issues were not at stake.

Attempts to keep the English crown in Protestant hands failed and in August of 1553 the Roman Catholic Mary Tudor entered London. Many of the outspoken Protestants were taken captive and imprisoned. Knox was able to escape from the country to Geneva, Switzerland.

It was during this time that Knox developed a theology of resistance to tyranny. He began smuggling pamphlets into England. The most significant of these was the *Admonition to England* (for complete title see *References* in the back of this book), published in July of 1554. With this move, he had stepped into new territory, going further than any Reformer had previously gone. Within a few years, tens of thousands of Huguenots were offering armed resistance to the French government; and the year Knox died saw the beginning of the successful revolt and saving of Holland. Knox had shocked the world with his *Admonition to England,* but he had also been convincing. Jasper Ridley in *John Knox* writes, "The theory of the justification of revolution is Knox's special contribution to theological and political thought."[3]

Whereas Reformers such as Martin Luther and John Calvin had reserved the right to rebellion to the civil rulers alone, Knox went further. He maintained that the common people had the right and duty to disobedience and rebellion if state officials ruled contrary to the Bible. To do otherwise would be rebellion against God.

Knox was not against civil government *per se.* He knew well that civil government is ordained of God. Knox maintained, however, that state officials have the duty of obeying God's Laws. He wrote: "Kings then have not an absolute power in their regiment to do what pleases them; but their power is limited by God's word."[4] A ruler must consider that he is "Lieutenant to One whose eyes watch upon him."[5] All life and all actions, he reiterated, must have their base in God's Word.

Knox finally arrived back in Scotland on May 2, 1559. Scotland became a Protestant country. The effectiveness of the Presbyterian system there was so great that the persecutions of the following century were unable to root it out. The Reformation had come to stay. And it was John Knox, an exponent of godly resistance in the face of tyranny, who planted the seeds that were later nurtured by such men as Samuel Rutherford.

In contrast to the countries named above where there was success for the Reformation—in each case involving various forms of civil disobedience or armed rebellion—one can think of where the Reformation was exterminated by force because of the lack of such protection:

Hungary: The Reformation had great initial success. But when the Turks pulled out of the country, the Roman Catholic authorities had unchecked power and used it to eliminate the Reformation—largely by killing off just about all of the Protestants.

France: The Huguenots were most successful in numbers and position. But on St. Bartholomew's Day (1572), lacking protection, the Reformation was broken in France by the mass assassination of most of its leadership.

Spain: There was a small Reformation movement among the monks of Seville. Lacking any protection, they were totally eliminated by martyrdom.

Thus, in almost every place where the Reformation flourished there was not only religious noncompliance; there was civil disobedience as well.

It was in this setting that Samuel Rutherford (1600-1661) wrote his *Lex Rex: or The Law and the Prince* (1644). What is the concept in *Lex Rex?* Very simply: The law is king, and if the king and the government disobey the law they are to be disobeyed. And the law is founded on the Law of God. *Lex Rex* was outlawed in both England and Scotland. The parliament of Scotland was meeting in order to condemn Samuel Rutherford to death for his views, and the only reason he was not executed as a civil rebel is because he died first.

In his classic work, *Lex Rex,* Rutherford set forth the proper Christian response to nonbiblical acts by the state. Rutherford, a Presbyterian, was one of the Scottish commissioners at the Westminster Assembly in London (1643-1647) and later became Rector at St. Andrews University in Scotland. The book *Lex Rex,* in a society of landed classes and monarchy, created an immediate controversy.

The governing authorities were concerned about *Lex Rex* because of its attack on the undergirding foundation of seventeenth century political government in Europe—"the divine right of kings." This doctrine held that the king or state ruled as God's appointed regent and, this being so, the king's word was law. Placed against this position was Rutherford's assertion that the basic premise of civil government and, therefore, law, must be based on God's Law as given in the Bible. As such, Rutherford argued, all men, even the king, are *under* the Law and not above it. This concept was considered political rebellion and punishable as treason.

Rutherford argued that Romans 13 indicates that all power is from God and that government is ordained and instituted by God. The state, however, is to be administered according to the principles of God's Law. Acts of the state which contradicted God's Law were illegitimate and acts of tyranny. Tyranny was defined as ruling without the sanction of God.

Rutherford held that a tyrannical government is always immoral. He said that "a power ethical, politic, or moral, to oppress, is not from God, and is not a power, but a licentious deviation of a power; and is no more from God, but from sinful nature and the old serpent, than a license to sin."[6]

Rutherford presents several arguments to establish the right and duty of resistance to unlawful government.[7] *First,* since tyranny is satanic, not to resist it is to resist God—to resist tyranny is to honor God. *Second,* since the ruler is granted power conditionally, it follows that the people have the power to withdraw their sanction if the proper conditions are not fulfilled. The civil magistrate is a "fiduciary figure"—that is, he holds his authority in trust for the people. Violation of the trust gives the people a legitimate base for resistance.

It follows from Rutherford's thesis that citizens have a *moral* obligation to resist unjust and tyrannical government. While we must always be subject to the *office* of the magistrate, we are not to be subject to the *man* in that office who commands that which is contrary to the Bible.

Rutherford offered suggestions concerning illegitimate acts of the state. A ruler, he wrote, should not be deposed merely because he commits a single breach of the compact he has with the people. Only when the magistrate acts in such a way that the governing structure of the country is being destroyed—that is, when he is attacking the fundamental structure of society—is he to be relieved of his power and authority.

That is exactly what we are facing today. The whole structure of our society is being attacked and destroyed. It is being given an entirely opposite base which gives exactly opposite results. The reversal is much more total and destructive than that which Rutherford or any of the Reformers faced in their day.

CHAPTER EIGHT
The Use of Civil Disobedience

Civil disobedience is, of course, a very serious matter and it must be stressed that Rutherford was the very opposite of an anarchist. In *Lex Rex* he does not propose armed revolution as an automatic solution. Instead, he sets forth the appropriate response to interference by the state in the liberties of the citizenry. Specifically, he stated that if the state deliberately is committed to destroying its ethical commitment to God then resistance is appropriate.

In such an instance, for *the private person*, the individual, Rutherford suggested that there are three appropriate levels of resistance: *First*, he must defend himself by protest (in contemporary society this would most often be by legal action); *second*, he must flee if at all possible; and, *third*, he may use force, if necessary, to defend himself. One should not employ force if he may save himself by flight; nor should one employ flight if he can save himself and defend himself by protest and the employment of constitutional means of redress. Rutherford illustrated this pattern of resistance from the life of David as it is recorded in the Old Testament.

On the other hand, when the state commits illegitimate acts against *a corporate body*—such as a duly constituted state or local body, or even a church—then flight is often an impractical and unrealistic means of resistance. Therefore, with respect to a corporate group or community, there are two levels of resistance: remonstration (or protest) and then, if necessary, force employed in self-defense. In this respect, Rutherford cautioned that a distinction must be made between a lawless uprising and lawful resistance.

For *a corporate body* (a civil entity), when illegitimate state acts are perpetrated upon it, resistance should be under the protection of the duly constituted authorities: if possible, it should be under the rule of the lesser magistrates (local officials). Rutherford urged that the *office* of the local official is just as much from God as is the *office* of the highest state official. Rutherford said, "When the supreme magistrate will not execute the judgment of the Lord, those who made him supreme magistrate, under God, who have under God, sovereign liberty to dispose of crowns and kingdoms, are to execute the judgment of the Lord, when wicked men make the law of God of none effect."

Samuel Rutherford and Bob Dylan would have understood each other. In "When You Gonna Wake Up" from the album *Slow Train Coming,*[1] Dylan has the lines:

Adulterers in churches and pornography in the schools
You got gangsters in power and lawbreakers making rules

When you gonna wake up,
When you gonna wake up,
When you gonna wake up
And strengthen the things that remain?

The difference in the centuries, and the difference in the language used, changes nothing.

In a similar way John Locke (1632-1704) approached the same problem. Locke took Rutherford's *Lex Rex* and secularized it. Locke, though secularizing *Lex Rex* and the Presbyterian tradition, nevertheless drew heavily from it. Locke made four basic points:

1. inalienable rights;
2. government by consent;
3. separation of powers;
4. the right of revolution (or you could word it, the right to resist unlawful authority).

These were the four points of Locke which were acted

upon by the men among the American Founders who followed Locke.

Witherspoon certainly knew Samuel Rutherford's writing well. The other Founding Fathers may have known him. They certainly knew about Locke. And for both *Lex Rex* and Locke there comes a time when there must be civil disobedience *on the appropriate level.* One begins not on the highest level, but on the appropriate level at one's own point of history.

Many within the Christian community would agree that Christians can protest and take flight in the face of state oppression. However, force of any kind is a place where many Christians stop short.

Force, as used in this book, means *compulsion* or *constraint* exerted upon a person (or persons) or on an entity such as the state.

When discussing force it is important to keep an axiom in mind: always before protest or force is used, we must work for reconstruction. In other words, we should attempt to correct and rebuild society before we advocate tearing it down or disrupting it.

If there is a legitimate reason for the use of force, and if there is a vigilant precaution against its over-reaction in practice, then at a certain point a use of force is justifiable. We should recognize, however, that overreaction can too easily become the ugly horror of sheer violence. Therefore, the distinction between force and violence is crucial. Os Guinness in *The Dust of Death* writes:

Without such a distinction there can be no legitimate justification for authority or discipline of any kind, whether on a parental or on a presidential level. In a fallen world the ideal of legal justice without the exercise of force is naive. Societies need a police force, a man has the right to defend his wife from assault. A feature of any society which can achieve a measure of freedom within form is that responsibility implies discipline. This is true at the various structural levels of society—in the sphere of the state, business, the community, the school, respectively.[2]

In a fallen world, force in some form will always be necessary. We must not forget that every presently existing government uses and must use force in order to exist. Two principles, however, must always be observed. *First,* there must be a legitimate basis and a legitimate exercise of force. *Second,* any overreaction crosses the line from force to violence. And unmitigated violence can never be justified.

As Knox and Rutherford illustrate, however, the proper use of force is not only the province of the state. Such an assumption is born of naiveté. It leaves us without sufficient remedy when and if the state takes on totalitarian dimensions.

One factor today that is different from Rutherford's day is that due to the immense power of the modern state there may be no place to flee. The Pilgrims could escape tyranny by fleeing to America. But today this is often much more complicated and for many in the world today the frontiers are closed.

At this time in our history, protest is our most viable alternative. This is because in our country the freedom that allows us to use protest to the maximum still exists. However, we must realize that protest is a form of force. This is very much so with the so-called "nonviolent resistance." This was, and is, not a negation of force, but a choice of the kind of force to be used.

In our day an illustration for the need of protest is tax money being used for abortion. After all the normal constitutional means of protest had been exhausted, then what could be done? At some point protest could lead some Christians to refuse to pay some portion of their tax money. Of course, this would mean a trial. Such a move would have to be the individual's choice under God. No one should decide for another. But somewhere along the way, such a decision might easily have to be faced. Happily, at the present time in the United States the Hyde Amendment has removed the use of national tax money for abortions, but that does not change the possibility that in some cases such a protest would be the only way to be heard. One can think, for example, of the tax money going to Planned Parenthood which is openly a propaganda agency for abortion.

Another illustration would be Christian schools resisting the undue entanglement and interference of the state into their affairs. This same thing is equally true for other private schools. That might include resisting the Internal Revenue Service's use of its tax rulings if they were used to enforce such undue entanglement and interference. Again there would be trials and possibly jail for someone. But at a certain point there may be no other effective protest.

The problem in relation to a state public school system is not just an abstract possibility. As I write, a case of undue entanglement and interference is in the courts in a situation that corresponds exactly to Samuel Rutherford's concept of the proper procedure for *a corporate body* to resist.

The state of Arkansas has passed a law allowing creation to be taught in the public schools. The American Civil Liberties Union (ACLU) is trying to have this law revoked, saying it violates the separation of church and state.

Here is a clear case fitting Rutherford's criteria. The state of Arkansas has passed a law. The courts are being used by the ACLU to try to nullify a state law which has the support of the original meaning of the First Amendment. The ACLU is arguing its case based upon a certain concept of the separation of church and state. But it must be stressed that this concept is entirely new and novel from the viewpoint of the original intent of the First Amendment and the total intent of the Founding Fathers. This new separation concept is a product of the recent humanist dominance in the United States and is being used in this case to destroy the power of a properly elected state legislature's "sovereign" ruling.

The ACLU is acting as the arm of the humanist consensus to force its view on the *majority* of the Arkansas state officials.

If there was ever a clearer example of the lower "magistrates" being treated with tyranny, it would be hard to find. And this would be a time, if the appeal courts finally rule tyrannically, for the state government to protest and refuse to submit. This fits Rutherford's proper procedures exactly.

It is a time for Christians and others who do not accept the narrow and bigoted humanist views rightfully to use the appropriate forms of protest.

In this case in Arkansas the ACLU has shown that it is the reverse of a civil liberties union. It is trying to make the schools totally secularistic, against the majority wishes of the Arkansas Legislature, and probably the majority of the citizens of the state of Arkansas. Under the guise of "civil liberties" it is tyranny, and not only the individual states should resist but the people should resist. The Humanist forces have used the courts rather than the legislatures because the courts are not subject to the people's thinking and expression by the election process—and especially they (the courts) are not subject to reelection. This is also related to the courts increasingly making law and thus the diminishing of the Federal and state legisla-

110

tures. The people must act against tyranny by returning these issues to themselves. The *Time* magazine
article of January 18, 1982 reporting on the lower
courts ruling against the Arkansas legislature spoke of
"a poll showing that 76 percent of the United
States public favors the teaching of both theories"—
i.e., evolution and creation. Thus if the poll is accu-
rate, the lower court's ruling is openly contrary to
the will of not only the legislature of Arkansas and
the people of Arkansas but to 76 percent of the
United States population. Any election figure getting
such a percentage would consider this a mandate.
Surely, the Founding Fathers would have considered
this situation to be tyranny. It would be appropriate to
remember the Boston Tea Party of December 16,
1773.

In a different area from the state schools: "undue
entanglement" in the Christian schools makes an
especially apt illustration. In Russia the state schools
are geared to teach their form of state religion—the
materialistic, humanistic world view—as the exclusive
position. And simultaneously one of the outstanding
issues in Russia concerning which Christians must disobey the state to be loyal to God is the state's laws
against the parents' teaching their children concerning Christ and Christian truth.

In the United States the materialistic, humanistic
world view is being taught exclusively in most state
schools. But then, those holding the humanistic world

111

view move to control (through the curricula and other ways) the Christian or other private schools—even though these schools were set up at private cost by the parents in order to give their children an education based on the world view of a universe created by a God who objectively exists.

There is an obvious parallel between this and the situation in Russia. And we really must not be blind to the fact that indeed in the public schools in the United States all religious influence is as forcibly forbidden as in the Soviet Union. Marxism usually is not taught here, but the total exclusive secularization is as complete. It should be noted that this is not only a problem for Christians but for other religious groups.

We must never forget that the humanistic position is an exclusivist, closed system which shuts out all contending viewpoints—especially if these views teach anything other than relative values and standards. Anything which presents absolute truth, values, or standards is quite rightly seen by the humanist to be a total denial of the humanistic position.

As a result the humanistic, material-energy, chance world view is completely intolerant when it presents itself through the political institutions and especially through the schools. In his book *Leftism*, Erik von Kuehnelt-Leddihn writes that as humanism begins to dominate the state "religion is then removed from the market place and the school, later from other domains of public life. The state will not tolerate any gods besides itself."[3] The school is their special target.

This is readily apparent in the Soviet Union. And it is carried forth in the name of religious freedom. For example, the Soviet Constitution provides:

Art. 124. In order to ensure to citizens freedom of conscience, the church in the U.S.S.R. is separated from the State, and the school from the church. Freedom of religious worship and freedom of anti-religious propaganda is recognized for all citizens.

Though this is clearly apparent in Russia in regard to its schools, it is also apparent in the public schools of the United States. The humanistic, material-energy, chance world view intolerantly uses every form of force at its disposal to make its world view the exclusive one taught in the schools.

One of the unhappy things in our country is that when states have objected to the continued encroachment on the original rights of the individual states, the objection has usually been motivated by some selfish end. However, if this could be put aside and the matter considered objectively, then we must realize that the individual states, in the origin of the United States, did not trust an overly powerful Federal Government, and the Constitution limited the Federal Government to definite areas. It was understood that powers not specifically granted to the Federal Government were not its prerogative.

James Madison (1751-1836) in *The Federalist*, no.

45, wrote: "The powers delegated by the proposed Constitution to the federal government are few and defined. Those which remain in the state governments are numerous and indefinite." In the intervening years this has been totally reversed.

Having lived in Switzerland for thirty-three years, I am especially sensitive to this. The individual Swiss cantons have courageously resisted the growth of Federal encroachment in Switzerland much more resolutely than the states have in the United States. Thus, the checks and balances in government between canton and Federal Government are functioning for governmental freedom in Switzerland much better than those between the individual states and the Federal Government in the United States. In our day, the checks and balances in government which resulted from the Reformation are functioning in this regard more consistently in Switzerland than they are in the United States. In Switzerland, federal statism has thus been somewhat restrained.

We must realize that the Reformation world view leads in the direction of government freedom. But the humanist world view with inevitable certainty leads in the direction of statism. This is so because humanists, having no god, must put something at the center, and it is inevitably society, government, or the state. Russia is the perfect example. But with the weakening or loss of the Christian consensus the Reformation countries have also become an example—including the

114

United States. Thus, if the United States is to move back toward the original Reformation basis, this would mean severely limiting the scope of Federal State authority.

It is curious that the present Socialist Government in France, out of sheer pragmatism, is trying to dismantle its overly centralized government. It may be only pragmatic and "political," but it is instructive. This overcentralization is the outgrowth of Napoleon's Governmental Code. They are trying to dismantle the authoritarian result which was produced by the chaos caused by the French Revolution. These results of chaos and then Napoleon's resulting authoritarian regime with its network of administrative bureaucracy were the very opposite of that which was produced by the American Revolution on its base which placed God above the government.[4] It is worth repeating James Madison's statement concerning the purpose of the United States Constitution: "The powers delegated by the proposed Constitution to the federal government are few and defined. Those which remain in the state governments are numerous and indefinite." But as the Judeo-Christian consensus in the United States has weakened and all but disappeared, with lack of vision even from a pragmatic perspective, let alone principle, the United States federal government has continually taken over the very power the original government of the United States did its best to curtail, limit, and resist.

115

Again we must see that what we face is a totality and not just bits and pieces. It is not too strong to say that we are at war, and there are no neutral parties in the struggle. One either confesses that God is the final authority, or one confesses that Caesar is Lord.

CHAPTER NINE

The Use of Force

There does come a time when force, even physical force, is appropriate. The Christian is not to take the law into his own hands and become a law unto himself. But when all avenues to flight and protest have closed, force in the defensive posture is appropriate. This was the situation of the American Revolution. The colonists used force in defending themselves. Great Britain, because of its policy toward the colonies, was seen as a foreign power invading America. The colonists defended their homeland. As such, the American Revolution was a conservative counter-revolution. The colonists saw the British as the revolutionaries trying to overthrow the legitimate colonial governments.

A true Christian in Hitler's Germany and in the occupied countries should have defied the false and counterfeit state and hidden his Jewish neighbors from the German SS Troops. The government had abrogated its authority, and it had no right to make any demands.

This brings us to a current issue that is crucial for the future of the church in the United States—the issue of abortion. What is involved is the whole issue of the value of human life. A recent report indicates that for every three live births, one child is aborted. Christians must come to the children's defense, and Christians must come to the defense of human life as such.

This defense should be carried out on at least four fronts:

First, we should aggressively support a human life bill or a constitutional amendment protecting unborn children.

Second, we must enter the courts seeking to overturn the Supreme Court's abortion decision.

Third, legal and political action should be taken against hospitals and abortion clinics that perform abortions.

In order to operate, many hospitals and abortion clinics receive tax money in some form—at least from individual states. Our representatives must be confronted with political force (if they will not do so out of principle) into introducing legislation cutting off such funds. If this fails, then lawsuits should be initiated to stop such funds from flowing to such institutions.

Simultaneously with these steps, some Christians have picketed. I greatly admired Dr. William S. Barker, President of Covenant Theological Seminary in St. Louis, when he supported seminary students who had been arrested for picketing an abortion clinic in St. Louis. The Covenant Seminary students said:

"We feel we owe the Covenant community an explanation. First, we consulted a lawyer on what is the most effective way to combat this problem; according to him, it is through being arrested which most effectually draws attention to the situation.

"Second, we wanted to demonstrate to the media and to the courts that abortion is not primarily a Catholic issue.

"Third, we felt the need to demonstrate our commitment in the view of the media and the pro-life organizations. We felt our Christian testimony was at stake here.

"Finally, we wanted to get involved in the court system: our case will receive a trial and could possibly be taken to higher courts. If abortion is to be eradicated, it will have to be through the proper legal means.

"It was not an easy decision to be disobedient to the magistrates, but in light of the facts—the destroying of human life on a grand scale—we felt this was the most effective way to respond. It is an urgent situation which requires response now."[1]

Dr. Barker acknowledged some differences within the seminary community but explained that he personally supported the students:

"Such non-violent civil disobedience is proper, I believe, when other channels have been exhausted or will not serve

119

to avoid or oppose the evil which one finds he cannot in obedience to God ignore or tolerate. At the same time one who violates man's law must be prepared to suffer the consequences."[2]

Fourth, the State must be made to feel the presence of the Christian community.

State officials must know that we are serious about stopping abortion, which is a matter of clear principle concerning the babies themselves and concerning a high view of human life. This may include doing such things as sit-ins in legislatures and courts, including the Supreme Court, when other constitutional means fail. We must make people aware that this is not a political game, but totally crucial and serious. And we must also demonstrate to people that there is indeed a proper bottom line. To repeat: the bottom line is that at a certain point there is not only the right, but the duty, to disobey the state.

Of course, this is scary. There are at least four reasons why.

First, we must make definite that we are in no way talking about any kind of a theocracy. Let me say that with great emphasis. Witherspoon, Jefferson, the American Founders had no idea of a theocracy. That is made plain by the First Amendment, and we must continually emphasize the fact that we are not talking about some kind, or any kind, of a theocracy.

In the Old Testament there was a theocracy commanded by God. In the New Testament, with the church being made up of Jews and Gentiles, and spreading over all the known world from India to Spain in one generation, the church was its own entity. There is no New Testament basis for a linking of church and state until Christ, the King returns. The whole "Constantine mentality" from the fourth century up to our day was a mistake. Constantine, as the Roman Emperor, in 313 ended the persecution of Christians. Unfortunately, the support he gave to the church led by 381 to the enforcing of Christianity, by Theodosius I, as the official state religion. Making Christianity the official state religion opened the way for confusion up till our own day. There have been times of very good government when this interrelationship of church and state has been present. But through the centuries it has caused great confusion between loyalty to the state and loyalty to Christ, between patriotism and being a Christian.

We must not confuse the Kingdom of God with our country. To say it another way: "We should not wrap Christianity in our national flag."

None of this, however, changes the fact that the United States was founded upon a Christian consensus, nor that we today should bring Judeo-Christian principles into play in regard to government. But that is very different from a theocracy in name or in fact.

Second, it is frightening when we realize that our consideration of these things, and this book, will certainly get behind the Iron Curtain and into other tyrannical countries where Christians face these questions in practice every day of their lives, in prison or out of prison. Their position is very different from ours. We have freedom from physical oppression and they do not.

The early church carried out their civil disobedience in the only way available to them. They came to the clear issue of worshipping Caesar or not, and rebelled in refusing to do so, though they knew the cost.

It seems to me that in most of the Iron Curtain countries the Christians are in about the same position as the early church. They are not in a position to change the system because of their low numbers, because as Christians they are systematically shut out of places of influence, and because of the iron control. Thus they must resist, in the manner the early church did, when they are commanded to disobey God. An illustration would be the state's command not to give their children religious training. To do so is considered an act of civil disobedience under the Criminal Codes of the Soviet Union. Jan Pit in *Persecution: It Will Never Happen Here?* writes about one of the restrictions on religious freedom in Iron Curtain countries: "Christians are forbidden to teach religion to children; therefore Sunday schools and youth gatherings are not allowed. Even within the home, Christian training is not to take place."[3] That clearly disobeys God's commands—as well as the parents' deepest longings if in-

122

deed the parents believe Christ is the way of eternal life—and the law would have to be disobeyed. Civil disobedience in that case would be continuing the instruction and, if apprehended, paying the price of being sent to the labor camps in Siberia, which at times still means certain death, and certainly great suffering. The labor camps take the place of the lions.

In the communist countries and in other countries in Africa, etc., God's leading might be to further action as in Poland at the present time—or at some point to an even more violent action.

With their idea of the "Perfectibility of Man" the Soviet leaders expected the "New Man" to be brought forth by changed economic conditions. This, of course, has not happened. The Christians have the opportunity to show that Christ, and the Christian understanding of reality, can, and do, bring forth the "New Man"—not perfectly of course until Christ returns, but still in a substantial way, whereas the Soviets have failed. In order for Christians to show forth the New Man they must demonstrate a positive practice and exhibit a caring Christian community in the group and care beyond the Christian group. But showing forth the New Man also means a standing against the law of the state which would destroy the very things Christians should produce in society. The civil disobedience forced upon them by the tyranny of the state is an essential part of being the New Man, because to obey would destroy both what Christians should be and also what they should be producing in society.

Three things must be stressed for those in *all* totalitarian countries:

1. A platonic concept of spirituality which does not include all of life is not true biblical spirituality. True spirituality touches all of life, including things of government and law, and not just "religious things."

2. We who are outside of such countries must allow those in these countries to know what "the appropriate level" is in their time and place. We in our place of lesser physical danger must not heap guilt on them. That is not to say that some of them will not compromise, but that is their responsibility before God.

3. They should understand that there is *a bottom line* of civil disobedience on the appropriate level. They should recognize that this is biblical because any government that commands what contradicts God's Law abrogates its authority. It is no longer our proper legal government, and at that point we have the right, and the duty, to disobey it.

Third, speaking of civil disobedience is frightening because of an opposite situation from the second. That is, with the prevalence of Marxist thinking—and especially with the attempted synthesis of Marxism and Christianity in certain forms of liberation theology in South America and other places—what we are saying could become a Marxist and terrorist tool to bring anarchy. Or in a similar vein, it could become a tool to impose by force the humanist world view resulting in the loss of humanness and in some form of authoritarianism.

Much of liberation theology is built on the concept of Man being basically good, linked with the idea that all people need is to be released from their economic chains. This is utopian, because Man is not basically good (bound only by social, economic, and political chains). Man is fallen. The Perfectibility of Man was the basis of much of the Enlightenment and of the French Revolution. Theoretically it was a basis of the Marxist-Lenin revolution in Russia. Each place this concept of the Perfectibility of Man has been acted on it has led to tragedy, to political chains, and to the loss of humanness.[4] Every attempt to put this utopian concept into practice has led to failure because it is false to what Man as he now is, really is. Man is not intrinsically unselfish, corrupted only by outward circumstances. He is fallen; he is not what he was created to be.

Even if some in this general stream of thought do not go as far as to be infiltrated by Marxism and the concept of the Perfectibility of Man, there is still the danger of confusing the Kingdom of God with the socialistic program. Those who have this tendency also could misuse this book.

Even as we say this, however, we must also say that the use of the freedoms we do have does not remove from us the duty of *making* and *using* our possessions

125

with compassion. That is a Christian duty which the church has often not emphasized.[5] We can understand why some, reacting to the church's lack of emphasis concerning the proper compassionate use of possessions, then make the mistake of equating the Kingdom of God with a state program. Nevertheless, we should clearly recognize that those who do confuse the Kingdom of God with a socialistic program could misuse this book, and we must see that they do not do so.

And *fourth*, we must say that speaking of civil disobedience is frightening because there are so many kooky people around. People are always irresponsible in a fallen world. But we live in a special time of irresponsible people, and such people will in their unbalanced way tend to do the very opposite from considering the appropriate means at the appropriate time and place. Anarchy is never appropriate.

But these very real problems do not change the principle that the men of the Reformation and the Founding Fathers of the United States knew and operated on. This principle is that there is a *bottom line* that must be faced squarely if the state is not to become all-powerful and usurp God's primacy. We must recognize that there is a *bottom line if we are to have real freedom of thought and action at the present time—even if, happily, we never reach that bottom line.* If we have not faced the possibility of civil disobedience, if needed, our thinking and action at the present time will lack the freedom they should have. Locke understood that.

Without the possibility of his fourth point—the right to resist unlawful authority—the other three would have been meaningless.

All the problems which do indeed exist do not change the need of thinking about the possibility of civil disobedience. Let us remind ourselves that Jonathan Blanchard and Charles Finney in their day thought through and taught this bottom line in regard to the need for the abolition of slavery. They taught this facing the possibility that they might have to pay the price of going to jail, or more, if that was the result of civil disobedience.

The colonists followed Rutherford's model in the American Revolution. They elected representatives from every state who, by way of the Declaration of Independence, protested the acts of Great Britain. Failing that, they defended themselves by force.

The Declaration of Independence contains many elements of the Reformation thinking of Knox and Rutherford and should be carefully considered when discussing resistance. It speaks directly to the responsibility of citizens concerning oppressive civil government.

After recognizing man's God-given absolute rights, the Declaration goes on to declare that whenever civil government becomes destructive of these rights, "it is the right of the people to alter and abolish it, and institute new government, laying its foundation on such principles, and organizing its powers in such

127

form, as to them shall seem most likely to effect their safety and happiness." The Founding Fathers, in the spirit of *Lex Rex*, cautioned in the Declaration of Independence that established governments should not be altered or abolished for "light and transient causes." But when there is a "long train of abuses and usurpations" designed to produce an oppressive, authoritarian state, "it is their right, it is their duty, to throw off such government . . ."

Simply put, the Declaration of Independence states that the people, if they find that their basic rights are being systematically attacked by the state, have *a duty* to try to change that government, and if they cannot do so, to abolish it.

Numerous historians have noted the strong religious influence on the American Revolution. One such historian was Harvard professor Perry Miller. Professor Miller was a convinced atheist, but he probably knew the primary sources of colonial history better than anyone of his generation. He concluded in *Nature's Nation*: "Actually, European deism was an exotic plant in America, which never struck roots in the soil. 'Rationalism' was never so widespread as liberal historians, or those fascinated by Jefferson, have imagined. The basic fact is that the Revolution had been preached to the masses as a religious revival, and had the astounding fortune to succeed."[6]

The importance of America's clergy has been too often ignored as a primary factor in the coming revolution and the support of it. They were called the "black regiment"—referring to their clerical robes—of the revolution. Professor Miller's words are vitally important:

[We] still do not realize how effective were generations of Protestant preaching in evoking patriotic enthusiasm. No interpretation of the religious utterances as being merely sanctimonious window dressing will do justice to the facts or to the character of the populace. Circumstances and the nature of the dominant opinion in Europe made it necessary for the official statement [that is, Declaration of Independence] to be released in primarily "political" terms—the social compact, inalienable rights, the right of revolution. But those terms, in and by themselves, would never have supplied the drive to victory, however mightily they weighed with the literate minority. What carried the ranks of militia and citizens was the universal persuasion that they, by administering to themselves a spiritual purge, acquired the energies God has always, in the manner of the Old Testament, been ready to impart to His repentant children.[7]

And we must again remember the *Wall Street Journal's* statement about the place the earlier revivals had in America "that helped sow the seeds of the American Revolution."

The thirteen colonies concluded that the time had come and they disobeyed. We must understand that for Rutherford and Locke, and for the Founding Fathers, *the bottom line* was not an abstract point of conversation over a tea table; at a certain point it had to be acted upon. The thirteen colonies reached the bottom line: they acted in civil disobedience. That civil disobedience led to open war in which men and women died. And that led to the founding of the United States of America. There would have been no founding of the United States of America without the Founding Fathers' realization that there is *a bottom line*. And to them the basic *bottom line* was not pragmatic; it was one of principle.

Please read most thoughtfully what I am going to say in the next sentence: *If there is no final place for civil disobedience, then the government has been made autonomous, and as such, it has been put in the place of the Living God.* If there is no final place for civil disobedience, then the government has been put in the place of the Living God, because then you are to obey it even when it tells you in its own way at that time to worship Caesar. And that point is exactly where the early Christians performed their acts of civil disobedience even when it cost them their lives.

CHAPTER TEN

By Teaching, by Life, by Action

What does all this mean in practice to us today? I must say, I really am not sure all that it means to us in practice at this moment. To begin, however, it certainly means this: We have been utterly foolish in our concentration on bits and pieces, and in our complete failure to face the total world view that is rooted in a false view of reality. And we have not understood that this view of reality inevitably brings forth totally different and wrong and inhuman results in all of life. This is nowhere more certain than in law and government—*where law and government are used by this false view of reality as a tool to force this false view and its results on everyone.*

It is time we consciously realize that when *any office* commands what is contrary to God's Law it abrogates its authority. And our loyalty to the God who gave this law then requires that we make the appropriate response in that situation to such a tyrannical usurping of power. I would emphasize at this point that Samuel Rutherford was not wrong, he was right; it was not only in the seventeenth century in Scotland where he was right; it was not only in 1776 where he was right: he is right in our century.

All we have been saying is relevant for the present moment, and especially in such areas as abortion. You will remember, however, that the primary consideration we have been dealing with is the possibility that the window which is now open might close. But the *First Track* is based on the window being open at the moment and our taking advantage of it. *We must not be satisfied with mere words.* With the window open we must try to roll back the results of the total world view which considers material-energy, shaped by chance, as the final reality. We must realize that this view will with inevitable certainty always bring forth results which are not only relativistic, and not only wrong, but which will be inhuman, not only for other people, but for our children and grandchildren, and our spiritual children. It will always bring forth what is inhuman, for with its false view of total reality it not only does not have a basis for the uniqueness and dignity of the individual person, but it is totally ignorant as to what, and who, Man is.

As we think about these things, we must think about one other factor: Those who have the responsibility as Christians, as they live under Scripture, must not only take the necessary legal and political stands, but must practice all the possible Christian alternatives simultaneously with taking stands politically and legally. In *Whatever Happened to the Human Race?* we stress this in regard to abortion, infanticide, and euthanasia of the old—that Christians must not only speak and fight against these things, but then must show there are Christian alternatives. But it must not only be in regard to abortion, infanticide, and euthanasia that alternatives are practiced. They must be practiced in all areas. This is so, and especially so, even when it is extremely costly in money, time, and energy.

As a positive example, the Christian Legal Society has set up a service for mediating disputes. I would say that is a Christian alternative. In a number of places crisis pregnancy centers have been set up. That is a proper alternative. We should be practicing these alternatives in all areas even as we stand legally and politically against our present society's and government's wrong solutions for the ills of humanity. We indeed are to be humanitarians in living contrast to the inhumanity brought forth by materialistic humanism.

Now I must quickly say there are going to be people who say, "don't use the legal and political means, just show the Christian alternatives." That is absolutely utopian in a fallen world, and specifically in a world such as ours at the present moment. But while it is utopian to say, just use the Christian alternatives and do not use the political and legal means, on the other hand, it is also incomplete and wrong only to use the legal and political means without showing forth the Christian alternatives. It is incomplete in conviction and will be incomplete in results; and it is wrong to the reality of the God we say we are obeying.

If we do not practice the alternatives commanded in the Scripture we are not living under the Scripture. And if we do not practice *the bottom line* of civil disobedience on the appropriate level, when the state has abrogated its authority, we are equally not living under the Scripture.

I would conclude by summarizing this Manifesto as follows:

1. The Reformation in Northern Europe not only brought forth a clear preaching of the gospel, but also brought forth distinctive governmental and social results. Among these was a form-freedom balance in government with its series of checks and balances. There was great freedom without the freedom pounding the order of the society to pieces because it was contained by the Christian consensus.

2. In the middle of the last century, groups began to enter the United States in increasing number which did not have the Reformation base. These enjoyed the freedom, though their base would not have produced it.

3. The greatest shift came with the rise of the mate-

134

rial-energy, chance view of final reality. This view was completely contrary to that which had produced the form-freedom balance in the United States with its resulting great freedom. This mistaken view of what final reality is leaves no room for meaning, purpose, or values in the universe and it gives no base for law. This view brings forth its natural results in all fields, and these results are the opposite of the natural results of the final reality being the personal God.

The humanistically based view of final reality began to be influential in the United States about eighty years ago. Its control of the consensus has become overwhelmingly dominant in about the last forty years. The shift has affected all parts of society and culture, but most importantly it has come largely to control government and law. These, then, have become the vehicle for forcing this view (with its natural results) on the public. This has been true in many areas—including, especially, the way it has been forced on students in the schools. Media which almost entirely hold the same world view have added to all this.

4. The world view which produced the founding of the United States in the first place is increasingly now not allowed to exert its influence in government, in the schools, or in the public means of information.

The result of the original base in the United States gave the possibility of "liberty and justice for all." And while it was always far from perfect, it did result in liberty. This included liberty to those who hold other views—views which would not give the freedom. The material-energy, chance view has taken advantage of that liberty, supplanted the consensus, and resulted in an intolerance that gives less and less freedom in courts and schools for the view which originally gave the freedoms. Having no base for law, those who hold the humanist view make binding law whatever they personally think is good for society at the moment. This leads increasingly to arbitrary law and rulings which produce chaos in society and which then naturally and increasingly tend to lead to some form of authoritarianism. At that point what the country had in the first place is lost and dead.

5. What is now needed is to stand against that other total world view. We must see and make clear that it is not the truth of final reality; and we must understand and show that it is producing its own natural results which are opposite to those upon which the United States was founded. It is opposite to the great freedoms produced which everyone now enjoys. What is needed at this time is to take the steps necessary to break the authoritarian hold which the material-energy, chance concept of final reality has on government and law.

6. The result would be freedom for all and especially freedom for all religion. That was the original purpose of the First Amendment.

7. With this freedom Reformation Christianity

would compete in the free marketplace of ideas. It would no longer be subject to a hidden censorship as it is now. It can and would give out the clear preaching of God's "good news" for individuals, and simultaneously it is also the view which gives the consistent base for the form-freedom balance in government and society—the base which brought forth this country with its freedoms. It is the responsibility of those holding this view to show it to be unique (the truth of total reality) for individual salvation and for society—by teaching, by life, and by action.

For our offenses are many in your sight,
    and our sins testify against us.
Our offenses are ever with us,
    and we acknowledge our iniquities:
rebellion and treachery against the Lord,
    turning our backs on our God,
fomenting oppression and revolt [against God],
    uttering lies our hearts have conceived.
So justice is driven back,
    and righteousness stands at a distance;
truth has stumbled in the streets,
    honesty cannot enter.
Truth is nowhere to be found,
    and whoever shuns evil becomes a prey.
The Lord looked and was displeased
    that there was no justice.

He saw that there was no one,
  and he was appalled that there was no one to
  intercede.[8]

Wake up! Strengthen the things which remain,
  that are about to die,
For I have not found your deeds complete in the sight
  of my God.[9]

Notes

Chapter 1: The Abolition of Truth and Morality
[1]*Humanist Manifestos I and II* (New York: Prometheus Books, 1973).
[2]This must not be confused with the humanistic elements which were developing slightly earlier in the Renaissance. Francis A. Schaeffer, *How Should We Then Live?* (Old Tappan, NJ: Fleming H. Revell Co., 1976), pp. 58-78.
[3]See *How Should We Then Live?*, pp. 40 and 109.
[4]See Will and Ariel Durant's book, *The Lessons of History* (New York: Simon & Schuster, 1968), pp. 84-86.
[5]*American Law Review*, XIV, (1880), p. 233.
[6]*Harvard Law Review*, XL, (1918).
[7]Henry De Bracton, Translation of *De Legibus et Consuetudinibus* (Cambridge, Mass.: Harvard-Belknap, 1968).
[8]See James L. Fisk, *The Law and Its Timeless Standard* (Washington: Lex Rex Institute).
[9]See Will and Ariel Durant's *The Lessons of History*, pp. 70-75.

Chapter 2: Foundations for Faith and Freedom
[1]David Walker Woods, *John Witherspoon* (Old Tappan, NJ: Fleming H. Revell Co., 1906).
[2]Edward Corwin, *The Supreme Court as National School Board*, Law and Contemporary Problems, 14, (1949), pp. 3, 11-12.
[3]Herbert W. Titus, Professor of Law, O. W. Coburn School of Law, *Education, Caesar's or God's: A Constitutional Question of Jurisdiction.*

[4]ibid.
[5]ibid.
[6]ibid.
[7]To be published by David C. Cook, Elgin, IL, 1982.
[8]Franky Schaeffer V, "The Myth of Neutrality," *Plan For Action* (Old Tappan, NJ: Fleming H. Revell Co., 1980), p. 37. *Plan For Action* is an action handbook for *Whatever Happened to the Human Race?*.
[9]Terry Eastland, "In Defense of Religious America," *Commentary* (June 1981), p. 39.
[10]Quoted in Perry Miller, editor, *The Legal Mind in America* (New York: Doubleday, 1962), p. 178.
[11]Eastland, p. 41.

Chapter 3: The Destruction of Faith and Freedom
[1]See *How Should We Then Live?*, p. 217.
[2]ibid.
[3]William Bentley Ball is a partner of the law firm of Ball and Skelly of Harrisburg, Pennsylvania. He has been lead council in litigation in 20 states and has appeared before the Supreme Court in parental rights cases. He was chairman of the Federal Bar Association Committee on Constitutional Law, 1970-74.
[4]See *How Should We Then Live?*, chapters "The Rise of Modern Science" and "The Breakdown of Philosophy and Science," pp. 130-166.
[5]Durant, *The Lessons of History*, pp. 50 and 51.
[6]ibid.
[7]See Jacques Monod, *Chance and Necessity* (New York: Alfred A. Knopf, 1971).

Chapter 4: The Humanist Religion
[1]*Humanist Manifestos I and II* (New York: Prometheus Books, 1973).
[2]John W. Whitehead, *The Second American Revolution*.
[3]William B. Provine, "The End of Ethics?" in *Hard Choices* (a magazine companion to the television series *Hard Choices*) (Seattle: KCTS-TV, channel 9, University of Washington, 1980), pp. 2, 3.
[4]Charles Peters, *How Washington Really Works* (Reading, MA: Addison-Wesley Pub. Co., 1980), p. 17.
[5]See *How Should We Then Live?*, pp. 239-243.

Chapter 5: Revival, Revolution, and Reform
[1]Howard A. Snyder, *The Radical Wesley* (Downers Grove, IL: InterVarsity Press, 1980), pp. 86-87.

Notes

[2]Jeremy Rifkin, *Entropy* (New York: Viking, 1980), pp. 234-240.
[3]Francis A. Schaeffer, *Pollution and the Death of Man—The Christian View of Ecology* (Wheaton, IL: Tyndale House Publishers, 1970).
[4]Charles Finney, *Systematic Theology* (Minneapolis: Bethany Fellowship, Inc., 1976).
[5]Jonathan Kaufman, "Old Time Religion, An Evangelical Revival Is Sweeping the Nation But with Little Effect," *Wall Street Journal* (July 11, 1980).
[6]Franky Schaeffer V, *Addicted to Mediocrity* (Westchester, IL: Crossway Books, 1981), pp. 27-28.

Chapter 6: An Open Window
[1]Eastland, p. 42.
[2]See pp. 224-254.
[3]Robert L. Toms, Editorial, *Theology, News and Notes* (December 1980), pp. 18-19. Mr. Toms is a partner of Caldwell & Toms of Los Angeles. He is a former Corporations Commissioner of the State of California under Governor Reagan.
[4]ibid.
[5]Samuel E. Ericsson, *Clergy Malpractice: Constitutional and Political Issues* (The Center for Law and Religious Freedom, Washington, D.C., May 1981). Mr. Ericsson is Special Counsel, Washington, D.C., office for the Center for Law and Religious Freedom. He is a graduate of Harvard Law School. Happily, since this book was written the church has won this case, but other cases of a somewhat like nature will certainly arise.

Chapter 7: The Limits of Civil Obedience
[1]Francis Legge, *Forerunners and Rivals of Christianity from 330 B.C. to 330 A.D.*, vol. 1 (New Hyde Park, NY: University Books, 1964), p. xxiv.
[2]The following section on John Knox, pp. 95-101, draws upon material which first appeared in an essay by David H. Chilton in "John Knox," *Journal of Christian Reconstruction*, vol. 5 (Winter 1978-79), pp. 194-206; reprinted here with the permission of the author.
[3]Jasper Ridley, *John Knox* (New York: Oxford, 1968), p. 171.
[4,5]John Knox, *Works* (New York: AMS Press, Vol. vi, 1968), pp. 236-238.
[6]Samuel Rutherford, *Lex Rex, or, The Law and the Prince* (n.p., 1644), published in vol. 3, *The Presbyterian Armoury* (1846), p. 34.
[7]The following section on Samuel Rutherford, pp. 101-104, draws upon material which appeared in an essay by Richard Flinn in "Samuel

141

Rutherford and Puritan Political Theory," *Journal of Christian Reconstruction*, vol. 5 (Winter 1978-79), pp. 49-74.

Chapter 8: The Use of Civil Disobedience
[1]Bob Dylan, *Slow Train Coming* (New York: Special Rider Music, CBS, Inc., 1979).
[2]Os Guinness, *The Dust of Death* (Downers Grove, IL: InterVarsity Press, 1973), pp. 177-178.
[3]Erik von Kuehnelt-Leddihn, *Leftism: From de Sade and Marx to Hitler and Marcuse* (New Rochelle, NY: Arlington House, 1974), p. 427.
[4]See *How Should We Then Live?*, pp. 120-124.

Chapter 9: The Use of Force
[1]"Seminary Students Arrested for Abortion Clinic Protests," *Bulletin Newsupplement* (Asheville, NC: Perspective Press for the Reformed Presbyterian Church, Evangelical Synod, April 15, 1980).
[2]ibid.
[3]Jan Pit, *Persecution: It Will Never Happen Here?* (Orange, CA: Open Doors With Brother Andrew, 1981), pp. 42-43.
[4]See *How Should We Then Live?*, chapter 6, "The Enlightenment," pp. 120-128 and pp. 154-160.
[5]See *How Should We Then Live?*, pp. 113-119.
[6]Perry Miller, *Nature's Nation* (Cambridge, Mass.: Harvard-Belknap, 1967), p. 110.
[7]ibid.
[8]Isaiah 59:12-16a.
[9]Revelation 3:2 (combination of King James Version and New International Version).

References

Books, articles, films, and records mentioned in the text.

Ball, William Bentley, "Religious Liberty: The Constitutional Frontier," a paper given at the Christian Legal Society Conference, South Bend, Ind., April 1980.

Blackstone, William. *Commentaries on the Law of England.* Chicago: University Chicago Press, 1979.

Bracton, Henry De. *De Legibus et Consuetudinibus.* Cambridge, Mass.: Harvard-Belknap, 1968.

Bunyan, John. *Pilgrim's Progress.* (Many editions in print.)

Chilton, David H. "John Knox," *Journal of Christian Reconstruction,* Vol. 5, Winter 1978-79.

Durant, Will and Ariel. *The Lessons of History.* New York: Simon and Schuster, 1968.

————. *The Story of Civilization,* 10 vols. New York: Simon and Schuster, 1935-1967.

Dylan, Bob. *Slow Train Coming* (record). New York: CBS, Inc., 1979.

Ericsson, Samuel E. *Clergy Malpractice: Constitutional and Political Issues.* Washington, D.C.: The Center for Law and Religious Freedom, 1981.

Flinn, Richard. "Samuel Rutherford and Puritan Political Theory," *Journal of Christian Reconstruction,* Vol. 5, Winter 1978-79.

Finney, Charles. *Systematic Theology.* Minneapolis: Bethany Fellowship, 1976.

Fisk, James L. *The Law and Its Timeless Standard.* Washington, D.C.: Lex Rex Institute, 1981.

Guinness, Os. *The Dust of Death.* Downers Grove, Ill.: InterVarsity Press, 1973.

Humanist Manifestos I and II. New York: Prometheus Books, 1973.

Jackson, Jeremy. *No Other Foundation: The Church Through Twenty Centuries.* Westchester, Ill.: Crossway Books, 1979.

Knox, John. "A Godly Warning or Admonition to the Faithful in London, Newcastle, and Berwick," in *The Works of John Knox,* vol. 3. New York: AMS Press, 1966.

Kuehnelt-Leddihn, Erik von. *Leftism: From de Sade and Marx to Hitler and Marcuse.* New Rochelle, N.Y.: Arlington House, 1974.

References

Legge, Francis. *Forerunners and Rivals of Christianity from 330 B.C. to A.D. 330.* New Hyde Park, N.Y.: University Books, 1964.

Miller, Perry, ed. *The Legal Mind in America: From Independence to the Civil War.* Cornell, N.Y.: Cornell University Press, 1962.

Miller, Perry. *Nature's Nation.* Cambridge, Mass.: Harvard-Belknap, 1967.

Monod, Jacques. *Chance and Necessity.* New York: Knopf, 1971.

Peters, Charles. *How Washington Really Works.* Reading, Mass.: Addison-Wesley, 1980.

Pit, Jan. *Persecution: It Will Never Happen Here?* Orange, Calif.: Open Doors With Brother Andrew, 1981.

Plato. *Republic.* (Many editions in print.)

Provine, William B. "The End of Ethics?" in *Hard Choices* (a magazine companion to the television series *Hard Choices*). Seattle, Wash.: KCTS-TV, channel 9, University of Washington, 1980.

Ridley, Jasper. *John Knox.* New York: Oxford, 1968.

Rutherford, Samuel. *Lex Rex: Or the Law and the Prince.*

Sagan, Carl. *Cosmos,* a public television series.

Schaeffer, Francis A. *Escape From Reason.* Downers Grove, Ill.: InterVarsity Press, 1968.

_____. *He Is There and He Is Not Silent.* Wheaton, Ill. Tyndale House, 1972.

_____. *How Should We Then Live?* Old Tappan, N.J.: Revell, 1976.

————. *How Should We Then Live?* (film). Muskegon, Mich., 1976.

————. *Pollution and the Death of Man: The Christian View of Ecology.* Wheaton, Ill.: Tyndale House, 1970.

————. *The God Who Is There.* Downers Grove, Ill.: InterVarsity Press, 1968.

————, and Koop, C. Everett, M.D. *Whatever Happened to the Human Race?* Old Tappan, N.J.: Revell, 1979.

————, and Koop, C. Everett, M.D. *Whatever Happened to the Human Race?* (film). Los Gatos, Calif., 1979.

Schaeffer, Franky. *Addicted to Mediocrity.* Westchester, Ill.: Crossway Books, 1981.

————. *Plan for Action.* Old Tappan, N.J.: Revell, 1980.

————. *Reclaiming the World* (film). In process.

Snyder, Howard A. *The Radical Wesley.* Downers Grove, Ill.: InterVarsity Press, 1980.

Whitehead, John W. *The Second American Revolution.* Elgin, Ill.: David C. Cook, 1982.

Woods, David Walker. *John Witherspoon.* Old Tappan, N.J.: Revell, 1906.

Index

147

Index

73f.; Christians not to be defined by, 78; partial identity of with Liberalism, 77-8
Conspiracy, not cause of political and cultural situation in United States, 56
Constantine and Constantinianism, 121
Copernicus, 44
Counter-Reformation, 95, 98-9
Covenant Theological Seminary (St. Louis), anti-abortion stand of students at, 119-20
Creation, doctrine of, 19, 23
Creationism in schools, 109-11
Cronkite, Walter, interview of in *International Herald Tribune*, 59-61

Darwin, Charles, 57
Darwinianism. *See* Natural Selection
David (Israel's King) as model for resistance, 104
Declaration of Independence (1776), 31, 33, 38, 127-8, 129
Deism (in America), 128
Democracy, 55-6, 59-61
Denmark, Reformation in, 94
Dennis, Lane, 12
Dewey, John, 24
District of Columbia, Circuit Court of, 80
"Divine Right of Kings" theory, 100
Douglas, Mr. Justice, quoted, 35
Drugs, as ideology or escape, 75, 76, 78
Durant, Will and Ariel, 45; in *The*

Humanist, 45; *The Lessons of History*, 45, 139, 140, 143; *The Story of Civilization* of, 45, 143
Dylan, Bob, *Slow Train Coming*, 105, 141, 143

Eastland, Terry, article in *Commentary*, 39, 78, 140, 141
Ecology and Christianity, 66
Edinburgh (Scotland), Knox in, 96
Education. *See* Schools and education
Einstein, Albert, 57
Elitism, modern forms of, 11, 48, 49, 79f.
Emperor (Holy Roman) and the Reformation, 94
Energy. *See* Reality: Materialistic view of
England, 28, 65, 96, 99; Church of, 93; Crown of, 97. *See also* Common Law, The (English)
Enlightenment, The, 21, 24, 125
Ericsson, Samuel E., *Clergy Malpractice*, 86-7, 141, 143
Europe, 34; anarchism in, 75-6. *See also* North European culture
Euthanasia, 22, 46-7, 67, 133
Evangelical leadership in United States, 63-4, 67f., 75, 87
Existence, 19; nature of, 18

Faith, bases of, ch. 2 *passim*
Family, breakdown of, 17
Farel, William, and Swiss Reformation, 95
Finney, Charles: and abolitionism, 66, 127;

149

Index

Hughes, Mr. Justice, 55
Huguenots and Reformation in
France, 97
Human dignity. *See* Man: as made
in God's image
Humanism, 11, 23, 24, 110, 112,
133; effect on society, 29-30,
48-9, 70, 112; false use of
separation doctrine, 36f.; as a
religion, ch. 4 *passim*; and
theology, 21f.
Humanist Manifesto, The, I (1933)
and II (1973), 13, 20, 24, 53-4,
58-9, 139, 140, 144
Humanist Pioneer Award, The (to
the Durants), 45
Humanist Society, The, 24
Humanitarianism, 23, 133
Humanities, The, 23
Human Life Bill, 118
Hungary, Reformation in, 98-9
Huxley, Aldous, 20
Huxley, Julian, 20, 24
Hyde Amendment, 108

"Inalienable rights," 32-3, 42,
105, 129
India, 121
Individual, The, 20, 25, 30, 51,
132; and resistance to authority,
103-4
Industrial Revolution, The, and
the revivals, 64-5
Infanticide, 22, 67, 133
Ingram, Jim and Gail, 12
Iron Curtain, The, 122

Jackson, Dr. Jeremy, 10, 12; *No
Other Foundation* of, 11-2, 144

Jefferson, Thomas, 32, 120, 128
Jews, The, 86, 118, 121
John (the Apostle), 5
Journal of Christian Jurisprudence,
144
Judaeo-Christian world-view, 24,
57, 69, 70-1; decline of its
influence, ch. 3 *passim,* 55, 58,
71, 115; influence on law and
government, 27f., ch. 2 *passim,*
43, 44-5, 121
Justice, 137; as prior principle in
law and society, 28

Kaufman, Jonathan, article in
Wall Street Journal, 67, 129, 141
Kent, Chief Justice (New York
State Supreme Court), 37
Knox, John, 95f., 127; his
Admonition to England (in *Works*
of), 97, 141, 144; and Scottish
Reformation, 96f.; theory of
resistance of, 97f., 107
Koop, C. Everett: struggle over
nomination as Surgeon-
General, 74; and *Whatever
Happened to the Human Race?,*
10, 145
Kuehnelt-Leddihn, Erik von,
Leftism, 112, 141, 144

Lausanne (Switzerland),
anarchists in, 76
Law, 9, 10, 18, 20, 21, 24, 38, 51,
131; as arbitrary, 'sociological'
and humanistic, 10, 24, 26f.,
41, 48, 50, 69, 135, 136; as
divine or supreme, 28-9, 32, 61,
68, 99f.; and justice, 28; as
natural or secular, 38, 42

151

Index

Moses and the Law, 28, 39
Music, 9

Napoleon, 36-7; Code of, 115
Natural selection, principle of, 26-7, 57-8
Nature, natural law, 38
Netherlands, The: anarchists in, 76; Protestantism in, 94, 97
New Testament. *See* Bible
Newton (Isaac), 57
New York State, Supreme Court of, 37
New Zealand, 24-5
Nims, Jerry (and family), 10
North European culture and extensions thereof, 18, 24-5, 43
Northwest Ordinance, 37

Oberlin College, 66
Old Testament. *See* Bible
Ollon (Switzerland), 95
Order in universe, denial of, 58

Parliaments, medieval, 25
Penn, William, 34
Pennsylvania (Commonwealth), Supreme Court of, 37
Permissiveness, 17
Personal peace (and affluence), 77
Peter (the Apostle), 5, 91-2
Peters, Charles, *How Washington Works*, 60, 140, 145
Philosophy, 29, 44, 47
Pietism, unbiblical aspects and effects of, 12, 18f.
Pilgrim (Fathers), 107
Pit, Jan, *Persecution: It Will Never Happen Here?*, 122, 142, 145

Plato, *The Republic*, 29
"Platonic" spirituality, 18f., 63, 68, 124
Pluralism (in the United States), 46-7
Pornography, 17
Prayer, 59, 73-4, 75; in the schools, 85
Presbyterians(ism), 31, 98, 99, 105
Princeton University (College of New Jersey), 31
Protestant Christianity, 37-8
Provine, William B., *The End of Ethics?*, 140
Public schools (United States). *See* Schools and education
Public Television (Broadcasting) Service, in Washington, D.C., lack of objectivity of, 57, 59
Punk Rock and nihilistic anarchism, 76

Rationalism, 45; in America, 128
Reagan, Governor (Ronald), 141
Reality: materialistic view of and socio-political effects, 18, 20, 25f., 39, 44f., 48-9, 51, 53, 57-9, 70-1, 73, 87, 89-90, 111, 113, 125, 132, 134-5, 136; nature of, 18, 19, 136; totality of, 19, 20, 51, 61-2, 137
Reformation, 34, 46, 136-7; effects on law and government of, 25, 28-9, 44-5, 93f., 114, 126, 134
Reformed Presbyterian Church, Evangelical Synod, *Bulletin Newsupplement* of, (119), 142
Reformers (16th century), 5, 126

153

154

Index

Index